At Issue

Should the U.S. Do Business with China?

D1506743

Other Books in the At Issue Series:

At Issue

Should the U.S. Do Business with China?

Laura Egendorf, Book Editor

GREENHAVEN PRESS
A part of Gale, Cengage Learning

GALE
CENGAGE Learning·

Detroit • New York • San Francisco • New Haven, Conn • Waterville, Maine • London

Christine Nasso, *Publisher*
Elizabeth Des Chenes, *Managing Editor*

© 2009 Greenhaven Press, a part of Gale, Cengage Learning.

Gale and Greenhaven Press are registered trademarks used herein under license.

For more information, contact:
Greenhaven Press
27500 Drake Rd.
Farmington Hills, MI 48331-3535
Or you can visit our Internet site at gale.cengage.com

For product information and technology assistance, contact us at

Gale Customer Support, 1-800-877-4253
For permission to use material from this text or product, submit all requests online at
www.cengage.com/permissions

Further permissions questions can be emailed to permissionrequest@cengage.com

Articles in Greenhaven Press anthologies are often edited for length to meet page requirements. In addition, original titles of these works are changed to clearly present the main thesis and to explicitly indicate the author's opinion. Every effort is made to ensure that Greenhaven Press accurately reflects the original intent of the authors. Every effort has been made to trace the owners of copyrighted material.

Cover image © Images.com/Corbis.

LIBRARY OF CONGRESS CATALOGING-IN-PUBLICATION DATA

Should the U.S. do business with China? / Laura Egendorf, book editor.
     p. cm. -- (At issue)
   Includes bibliographical references and index.
   ISBN 978-0-7377-4112-4 (hbk.)
   ISBN 978-0-7377-4113-1 (pbk.)
   1. United States--Foreign economic relations--China. 2. China--Foreign economic relations--United States. 3. United States--Commerce--China. 4. China--Commerce--United States. I. Egendorf, Laura K., 1973-
   HF1456.5.C6S56 2008
   337.73051--dc22
                                                             2008026076

Printed in the United States of America
2 3 4 5 6   12 11 10 09 08

ED311

Contents

Introduction

"Made in China" is one of the most ubiquitous labels on merchandise, and for most Americans, it is the extent of their economic interaction with China. For others, however, the Chinese economy has had a much more direct impact on their livelihoods. The outsourcing of American jobs, particularly jobs in the technology industry, to China has grown significantly in recent years, prompting questions as to whether it is beneficial to the U.S. economy.

In the past, most of the technology jobs that have left the United States have gone to India. However, the lower costs of doing business in China and the increase in college graduates among Chinese workers has led to a shift away from India. Research has shown that the cost of labor in China is 40 percent lower than in India. Prominent firms such as IBM and Microsoft are taking advantage of these reduced costs by placing information technology (IT) support in Shanghai and other Chinese cities. Despite these lower costs, India still has a considerable lead in revenue from IT outsourcing. According to an article in the *Los Angeles Times*, India's $18 billion in revenue in 2007 was six times greater than China's; China may not close the gap for another decade.

Many people hope that the move to outsourcing jobs to China is short-lived, because they believe that such corporate decisions are harmful to American workers. For companies, the benefit of outsourcing is obvious—an engineer in China commands a salary of $300 to $500 per month, just a fraction of what it would cost to hire an American. With as many as 200,000 Chinese students graduating each year with degrees in IT, according to Jacqueline Zhang in an August 2005 article at Sourcingmag.com, the pool for American companies to draw from has become substantial. Consequently, American workers can no longer count on the long-term security of a career in technology. Kathleen Madigan, the business outlook editor for *BusinessWeek*, writes, "As soon as work can be made routine—whether it's reading an X-ray or creating blueprints—the job can potentially be outsourced. That promises big, and often disquieting, changes ahead for many." Madigan suggests that rather than offer tax breaks to U.S. companies in exchange for not outsourcing jobs, U.S. government and businesses should focus more on improving the American educational system so that workers can learn cutting-edge technologies that will ensure them steady incomes.

Proponents of outsourcing argue that concerns over moving jobs to China are misguided because such business decisions benefit the U.S. economy. Daniel Griswold, director of the Center for Trade Policy Studies at the Cato Institute, writes, "According to a 2003 study by the McKinsey Global Institute, outsourcing delivers large and measurable benefits to the U.S. economy: It reduces costs for IT and other services by as much as 60 percent." In addition, the outsourcing of IT production and jobs may increase the U.S. economy by more than $60 billion per year. Supporters of outsourcing jobs to China also contend that IT outsourcing has little effect on America's college-educated workers, with wages rising and unemployment among that sector remaining low. Not surprisingly, the Chinese government is especially supportive of outsourcing; it offers foreign businesses a variety of incentives, such as waiving taxes and subsidizing the costs of training workers.

As the controversy over outsourcing shows, the economic ties between the United States and China are highly complex. In *At Issue: Should the U.S. Do Business with China?*, contributors analyze the benefits and drawbacks of this relationship. Trade and other economic interaction affect not only corporations and workers, but also consumers, the environment, and China's political system.

1

Trade with China Benefits the United States

Stephen Spruiell

Stephen Spruiell is a political reporter for National Review.

Congress has taken the wrong approach to the problem of unsafe products that are imported from China. Politicians seek to punish China with excessive tariffs. However, such legislation would make goods more expensive and lead to retaliatory tariffs. Congress should recognize that free trade helps the United States increase its influence in China and throughout Asia.

To Zheng Xiaoyu, it all must have seemed so unfair. Bribery is common in China and rarely punished. But, in America, reports about poisoned pet food and tainted toothpaste had activated a familiar chorus line of jerking knees on Capitol Hill, and the Chinese government was desperate to demonstrate its commitment to product safety. Zheng protested that his punishment was "too severe," an understandable complaint. To be shot in the head for taking a few hundred thousand dollars in bribes as China's top food and drug regulator? When William Jefferson, the Louisiana Democrat caught with $90,000 in his freezer, hasn't even lost all of his committee assignments? In China, of course, they do things differently. A mere four months after his arrest, Zheng was executed.

Stephen Spruiell, "Doing Their Duties: Congress Disguises Protectionism as China Indignation," *National Review*, vol. 59, no. 19, October 22, 2007, p. 40. Copyright © 2007 by National Review, Inc., 215 Lexington Avenue, New York, NY 10016. Reproduced by permission.

A Spate of Product Safety Bills

China's rapid and brutal handling of the Zheng affair made headlines around the world, but it did not stanch the flood of China-related legislation that has poured from the 110th Congress. Since he was put to death in mid-July [2007], lawmakers have introduced 24 such bills, bringing the total number of China-related bills introduced since January [2007] to 87. Twenty of those bills address concerns over product safety; most of the others stem from longstanding grievances over the value of China's currency or subsidies for its exporters. The fear now among free-traders—and Zheng's execution shows that the Chinese fear it too—is that Congress will use product safety as a rallying cry to pass a raft of legislation whose true aim is to punish China for competing too effectively against a handful of U.S. businesses.

It should be stated at the outset that any products imported into the United States should meet a minimum set of safety standards. U.S. companies typically develop in-house standards to protect their brands, but business arrangements involving long, complicated chains of foreign contractors and subcontractors demand more rigorous outside oversight. For instance, one recent product-safety scandal involved the U.S. toy giant Mattel, which had to recall 1.5 million toys after it learned that one of its contract manufacturers in China had used lead paint. (In a grim echo of the Zheng execution, the Chinese factory owner hanged himself.)

Congress could accomplish some legitimate improvements in product safety if it approached the subject in a restrained, rational manner.

[In spring 2007], before the lead-paint crisis, a spate of dead dogs and cats had pet-food makers initiating massive recalls across the U.S. When the killer ingredient turned out to be tainted wheat gluten from China, members of Congress started falling all over themselves to be the first to crack down on dangerous dog chow. Within weeks, Sen. Dick Durbin (D., Ill.) and Rep. Rosa DeLauro (D., Conn.) introduced the "Human and Pet Food Safety Act of 2007," directing the Food and Drug Administration to create a special certification program for any country wishing to export food products to the U.S.

Durbin then took it a step further and, in a bill called the Imported Food Security Act, proposed collecting user fees from food importers to pay for the new inspections regime. (His partner in the House this time was Rep. Marcy Kaptur, Democrat of Ohio, whose previous work on China this year [2007] included a proposal to cancel China's normalized trading status.) "User fees on importers" is a fancy way of saying tariffs; they have approximately the same effect. All of a sudden, a decent idea (create a certification program that includes overseas inspections of Chinese food factories and testing labs) acquired a distinct whiff of protectionism.

Congress Is Taking an Irrational Approach

This is unfortunate, because Congress could accomplish some legitimate improvements in product safety if it approached the subject in a restrained, rational manner. (A bill introduced by Rep. Mike Ferguson, Republican of New Jersey, to require third-party lead-paint checks has garnered the support of a battered toy industry eager to win back the public's confidence in time for the Christmas shopping season.) But look at the other trade bills that have come out of this Congress: Does this look like a group of lawmakers you can trust to handle an issue as sensitive as product safety without letting their protectionist impulses rage?

Take the bills that deal with currency. The currency issue has come to symbolize Congress's pig-headedness when it comes to trade with China. For several years now, an odd coalition of manufacturers, labor groups, and currency speculators has accused China of keeping its currency, the renminbi

(RMB), artificially undervalued in order to make its exports cheaper and undercut competitors abroad. The only way to deal with this problem, they say, is for Congress to pass legislation that threatens China with high retaliatory tariffs unless it stops "manipulating" its currency.

China experts who disagree with this view have countered that—even though China's large supply of foreign reserves appears to indicate that its currency should be stronger—China has kept the RMB from "floating" upward simply because it does not yet have the financial institutions in place to cope with wild swings in the valuation of its currency. Currency instability was at the root of the 1997–98 Asian financial crisis, and no one wants to see that happen in China at a time when the consequences could be far more severe.

In a 2005 paper for the Carnegie Endowment for International Peace, economist Albert Keidel, an expert on Chinese exchange-rate issues, laid out another explanation for China's rapid accumulation of foreign reserves. Currency speculators, Keidel wrote, were pouring money into China in the form of speculative bets on the RMB; that is, these speculators were buying Chinese currency with the expectation that the "float the currency" crowd in Washington would succeed in bullying China into letting the value of the RMB rise, at which point the speculators could cash out with a huge profit. Furthermore, said Keidel, if the "artificially undervalued" RMB is fueling China's trade surplus with the U.S., it should be fueling a trade surplus with China's other trading partners, too. But it's not: In fact, China runs a trade deficit with the rest of the world, mostly because it is importing parts from its Asian neighbors (and paying dearly for them, if its currency is truly undervalued) and then exporting finished products to us.

Tariffs Would Be Disastrous

Nor is China's currency a top concern for most of the U.S. business community. Erin Ennis, vice president of the U.S.–

China Business Council, says that in surveys of the council's 250-plus member companies, China's currency "is not the number-one issue for most companies doing business in or with China. There is a part of the business community that views that as its number-one issue. Saying that it's [the entire business community's] number-one issue is inaccurate."

Businesses on the council tend to have problems, such as finding qualified personnel in China, that Congress can do little about. But that doesn't mean Congress can't create problems for them: On [a 2006] survey, members expressed their concern that the political fallout from a legislative "solution" to the currency problem will have a negative impact on their business interests in China. That's the extent of their concerns about China's exchange rate.

[Tariffs on China] would violate our commitment as a member of the World Trade Organization.

As if to vindicate the businessmen's astuteness in analyzing how Congress works, lawmakers have crafted dozens of "solutions" this year that run the gamut from the mildly annoying to the spectacularly disastrous. On the disastrous end, Reps. John Spratt (D., S.C.) and Sue Myrick (R., N.C.) introduced a bill that would impose an across-the-board tariff of 27.5 percent on all imports from China if it does not revalue the RMB.

It's hard to overstate how harmful such a measure would be. First, it would violate our commitment as a member of the World Trade Organization [WTO] to refrain from slapping tariffs on whomever we feel like. Second, a tariff would have an immediate effect on the price of a wide swath of directly imported goods, as well as a residual effect on the price of American goods manufactured using Chinese imports, making both more expensive. Third, China would undoubtedly enact retaliatory tariffs—blocking access to our fastest-growing export market. Carolina textile manufacturers who are having difficulty competing with Chinese imports would see business improve, for a little while, until Turkey and Bangladesh ramped up production and offered consumers a cheaper alternative, at which point Reps. Spratt and Myrick would happily swoop down and deny them that choice as well.

Ohio Democrat Tim Ryan joined California Republican (and one-note presidential candidate) Duncan Hunter to create a slightly more nuanced but just as damaging approach called the Fair Currency Act of 2007. This bill would classify the "misalignment" in China's exchange rate as an export subsidy, thus exposing Chinese imports to what are known as countervailing duties.

Countervailing duties are tariffs that the Commerce Department is authorized to levy against subsidized imports in certain cases. These duties are regulated by the WTO, and there is little chance that the "Fair Currency Act" would pass WTO scrutiny if challenged. The WTO Agreement on Subsidies and Countervailing Measures stipulates that in order to impose countervailing duties, a country must be able to demonstrate a causal link between subsidized imports and injury to a domestic industry. We are nowhere near that point with China's exchange rate. How, exactly, among the wild tangle of factors affecting competition between Chinese imports and domestic products, is the Commerce Department supposed to isolate the effect of China's exchange rate and prove that that's what did the damage?

Trading with China gives us more leverage with the Chinese regime.

Finally, on the mildly annoying end, we find the bill by Sens. Max Baucus (D., Mont.) and Chuck Grassley (R., Iowa) designed to ratchet up the pressure on China until it floats the RMB. First, the bill takes away the treasury secretary's discretion to determine whether China is manipulating its currency and directs him instead to use a formula that is designed to yield such a finding. Once the treasury secretary declares China's currency to be "misaligned," China will have six months to revalue the RMB before a series of punitive measures sets in. These measures would include plugging China's exchange rate into a formula for determining antidumping duties, which are another form of tariff the U.S. can impose on subsidized imports. This provision would run into the same kind of trouble at the WTO that the Ryan-Hunter bill would: The relevant agreements do not consider favorable exchange rates a "subsidy."

Free Trade Increases Our Influence in Asia

The Baucus-Grassley bill stands the greatest chance of building the veto-proof majority any of these bills would need to become law, but it's still a long shot. What's most depressing about these bills is what they say about the political atmosphere of the current Congress. It is by all indications the most protectionist Congress of the last two decades, coming at a time when the U.S. has unprecedented opportunities to use free trade to expand our influence in the Asia-Pacific region. Put China aside for a moment and consider the U.S.–South Korea Free Trade Agreement, completed [June 2007] and awaiting a vote in Congress.

The U.S.-Korea pact would be the biggest of its kind since NAFTA [North American Free Trade Agreement], expected to expand trade between the countries by more than $20 billion. More important, it would strengthen ties between the U.S. and Korea at a time when such a move is needed to balance China's growing power. It is important for the stability of the region that China's rise continue peacefully. To that end, trading with China gives us more leverage with the Chinese regime than we would have if we shut China out of our markets. And building upon existing alliances with nearby Asian democracies reduces their economic dependence on China and acts as a check on China's hegemonic ambitions.

The renewal of the president's fast-track trade-promotion authority, which allows him to submit trade agreements to Congress for an up-or-down vote, would also increase our influence in the region. Fast-track, which expired on June 30, [2007,] would allow the administration a freer hand in solving some of the real problems plaguing companies doing business in China, from inadequate intellectual-property safeguards to increased market access for exporters.

The current Congress appears unlikely to take up either of these important tasks. It is holding up the Korea deal over concerns about market access for American beef and cars. As for the president's fast-track authority, the Democrats are loath to approve anything that might be interpreted as giving George W. Bush "more power"; Korea and fast-track will probably be battles for the next president to fight.

Which is a shame. Trade with China is a force for growth in our economy, and stronger ties with Korea are vital to our strategic interests in the Asia-Pacific region. Some U.S. businesses are struggling to compete with Chinese imports, but hundreds more are prospering thanks to freer trade with China. Manufacturers who import cheaper parts from China have seen the impact on their bottom lines, and, while the rate at which we buy things from China is increasing, the rate at which we sell things to China is increasing faster.

Trade with China Is Not to Blame for Job Loss

Protectionist lawmakers argue that our trade deficit with China (about a third of our total trade deficit) is too large. Its size is irrelevant, according to the non-partisan Congressional Budget Office. "The growth in trade that results from lowered trade barriers is generally beneficial regardless of its effects on the balance of trade," the CBO reported in a 2003 study. "It is the growth in both exports and imports of each country that allows production to shift to the most efficient producers and thereby expands output."

This "shift" is the real reason some lawmakers have gone to the mattresses. Although trade with China has boosted the gross domestic product, put downward pressure on prices, and done all this without increasing overall unemployment, it has also, according to a China Business Forum report released [in 2006], "contribut[ed] to a decades-long shift in the structure of U.S. employment away from manufacturing and toward services."

It's long past time for lawmakers from manufacturing districts to recognize two things. First: This jobs shift began before China was a major U.S. trading partner and for reasons that have more to do with productivity gains than trade. Manufacturing in the U.S. remains robust; we're doing an increasing amount of work with fewer workers.

The second is that free-traders are willing to meet them halfway on assistance to workers who can demonstrate that they lost their jobs to overseas competition, but only if it means more support for free-trade deals. Baucus introduced a bill in January [2007] that would expand trade-adjustment assistance, but so far he has offered nothing but antagonism on the issue of China. Why should we expand the subsidies if we're not expanding trade?

Unfortunately, these lawmakers may not be able to compromise anymore, even if they wanted to. Too many freshman Democrats either owe their seats to anti-trade rhetoric (Rep. Heath Shuler of North Carolina) or genuinely believe that free trade is destroying the country (Sen. Sherrod Brown of Ohio). Either way, the anti-trade Dems (and Republicans) form a powerful bloc in Congress that will prove difficult to overcome, and a glance at their long list of policy initiatives— from protectionism disguised as public safety to trade-adjustment assistance without trade—shows that they're determined not just to block trade agreements, but to play an active part in rolling back the expansions of trade we've seen over the past decade. A final sad aspect of the Zheng Xiaoyu affair is that his execution is unlikely to have its intended effect, at least in the U.S. Congress: Product safety is just the latest red herring from its growing cadre of protectionists.

2

China Uses Unfair Trade Practices

Benjamin L. Cardin

Benjamin L. Cardin is a Democratic senator from Maryland.

*China utilizes unfair trade practices that create economic prob-
lems for the United States. Among these practices are the manipulation of the Chinese currency, which makes Chinese exports
less expensive than U.S. exports, and the failure of the Chinese
government to protect American companies' intellectual property
rights. The United States must enforce fair-trade laws and pass
stronger legislation if it is to decrease its trade deficit with China.*

Chairwoman [Carolyn] Bartholomew and Vice Chair
[Daniel] Blumenthal, thank you both for the opportunity
to testify on U.S.-China relations and their implications for
economic and security cooperation.

Prior to my election in 2006 to the United States Senate, I
spent eighteen years on the House of Representatives Committee on Ways and Means. The last two years I served as the
ranking member of the Trade Subcommittee.

U.S.-China trade was a matter that often made its way on
the Subcommittee's agenda. There can be no mistake: China is
the fastest-growing economic force in the world today. China's
need for sources of energy and markets to absorb its products
means there are few nations in the world that have yet to be
impacted by China's largesse.

Benjamin L. Cardin, *The U.S.-China Relationship: Economics and Security in Perspec-
tive*, Hearing Before the U.S.-China Economic and Security Review Commission, One
Hundred Tenth Congress, First Session, February 1–2, 2007, pp. 11–13. www.uscc.gov.

The Result of Unfair Trade Practices

China is one of the most important trading partners of the United States, yet, there are severe problems with this relationship due to China's longstanding unfair trade practices. Their unfair trading practices have led to historic trade imbalances allowing China to acquire too large an amount of U.S. debt. That is not in our security or economic interest.

China's unfair trade practices include currency manipulation, flagrant piracy of intellectual property, unreasonable restrictions on market access and industrial subsidies.

The U.S. trade deficit with China has doubled in the last five years. This is a dangerous trend as it forces our nation to borrow massive amounts of money from foreign countries to fund the deficit. The imbalance is caused in part by China's continuing currency manipulation. Despite repeated promises to adopt a more flexible exchange rate, China continues to peg its currency to a rigid policy that has caused the yuan to be undervalued by as much as 40 percent. Thus, Chinese exports are cheaper than U.S. exports.

China also continues to [flout] international trade rules by failing to crack down on widespread pirating of intellectual property. Again, despite repeated commitments to protect and enforce intellectual property rights—in accord with the WTO [World Trade Organization]—every year more and more American companies lose an estimated $2 billion to Chinese copycats.

Additionally, China continues to use unfair trade practices to provide advantages to Chinese companies and restrict U.S. companies from competing on equal footing. China often imposes overly burdensome licensing and operating requirements and often discriminatory regulations to restrict U.S. exports of services.

More Aggressive Legislation Is Needed

In response to China's unfair trade practices, I introduced the Fair Trade with China Act of 2005 (FTCA). The FTCA addressed the four key facets of the U.S. trade relationship with China. [The bill did not become law.]

First, the FTCA amended the U.S. countervailing duty law to direct the Department of Commerce to investigate subsidies provided by the Chinese government to sectors of industry or agriculture.

Second, the FTCA proposed to change U.S. law to make currency manipulation an unjustifiable act, policy, or practice. Thereby, the USTR [United States Trade Representative] could file a case in the WTO to address currency manipulation.

Third, the legislation proposed strengthening the special China safeguard law, which is intended to provide a remedy for U.S. industries against import surges caused by China's nonmarket economy. Additionally, we proposed to amend the customs provisions to ensure the collection of duties owed on imports from China.

Fourth, the FTCA would revive the "Super 301" trade law to direct the USTR to identify the priority barriers to U.S. exports of goods and services and China's unfair trade practices. This would also include China's failure to protect intellectual property rights and unfair trade practices.

For America's economic and security interest, it is essential that we aggressively enforce fair trade laws with China and if necessary strengthen our enforcement provisions through congressional action.

China-Iran Relations Are a Concern

Another cautionary aspect of China's economic ascendancy is its relations with Iran. This relationship is both mutual dependence and political calculation.

China finds in Iran a permanent source for its exports and growing energy demand. China is the second-leading exporter of goods to Iran with 8.3 percent of total market share. Between 2000 and 2005, Iran's imports from China rose by 360 percent. In dollar value, this represents a leap from US$3.3

billion in trade to US$9.2 billion. Additionally, 13.6 percent of China's oil imports come from Iran.

There should be no surprise as to why China opposes sanctions against Iran for Iran's noncompliance with the international community regarding its nuclear energy program.

As long as China enjoys a United Nations Security Council veto authority, Iran finds that it has a very useful and powerful ally.

I believe the United States should include Iran's nuclear program in all high-level talks with China to ensure Iran is clear it cannot circumvent international compliance by hiding behind China's economic and political clout.

Again, I thank the Commission for an opportunity to testify, and I look forward to the final report on these hearings.

3

Economic Engagement Could Help Make China a Democracy

Taylor Wyman

Taylor Wyman is a former teaching assistant at the Heinz School of Public Policy and Management at Carnegie Mellon University in Pittsburgh.

Economic engagement is the best way for the United States to improve political conditions in China. Even though American companies might have to compromise their principles at times, such as Google allowing the censorship of Internet searches, these actions are acceptable because they are part of the long-term efforts of improving the living standards of the Chinese people. Other steps, in addition to economic engagement, that will improve political conditions in China include increasing bilateral interactions between the two nations and developing countercensorship technologies.

A large body of academic research supports the link between economic development and democratically protected human rights. Seymour Martin Lipset's seminal "Social Requisites for Democracy" (1959) first used statistical analyses to show a correlation. More recent scholarship has broadened the list of conditions supporting democracy from Lipset's original focus on wealth, industrialization, urbanization, and education. The need for a shift in the class power balance and the importance of information access are now also considered key prerequisites to political liberalization.

Taylor Wyman, "U.S.-China Foreign Policy Recommendations," *Heinz School Review*, vol. 3, no. 1, March 15, 2006. http://journal.heinz.cmu.edu. Reproduced by permission.

Political Reform Is a Lengthy Process

The U.S. Department of State has incorporated this research and long supported a policy of economic engagement with China that promotes the social conditions necessary for political reform. But recently two prominent American companies, Google and Yahoo! Inc. were the focus of media attention regarding Google's censorship of Chinese internet searches and Yahoo's revelation of a Chinese journalist's email information. Compromises by American businesses with the Chinese government are a necessary part of maintaining influence in China. Influence is necessary to raise living standards and provide access to information. Chinese political pressure on American companies and internet dissidents is not symptomatic of the failure of economic development to bring political reform, but rather evidence that the process is beginning to work.

The U.S. policy of economic engagement and the work of America's internet companies are helping to build the foundations of democratic change in China.

China was granted World Trade Organization (WTO) membership in 2001, . . . and when China is evaluated using the democratic prerequisites outlined above, it becomes evident that the impact of development is still in its early stages. With respect to wealth, China's per capita GDP [gross domestic product] has grown to an estimated $6200 in 2005, but it still ranks as lower-middle income among the world's nations, behind authoritarian regimes in Belarus and Iran, and $3800 less than democratic Costa Rica. Considering industrialization, industry and construction now represent over 50 percent of GDP, but 49 percent of the actual labor force, almost 400 million people, continue to work in agriculture. Since 1978, China's urban population has grown from 170 million to 453 million, but that still makes it only 31 percent urbanized, far less than the 78 percent found in wealthy democracies. In education, China's 90.9 percent literacy rate also falls below Lipset's benchmark of 96 percent for stable democracies. China had more than 100 million internet users accessing information in 2005, a figure second only to the U.S. but representing less than 8 percent of their population.

These statistics describe a China that has begun to develop the social conditions that promote political liberalization, but this process has a long way to go. Evidence of this development's impact on Chinese politics can be seen in increased citizen criticism of government actions during the SARS and avian flu outbreaks and, most recently, after a toxic spill on the Songhua River. More importantly, it can be seen in a recent report on China's cyber police by the organization Reporters Without Borders. They report that "people in China are better informed today than at any previous period in history" and that, due to the rise of net dissidents, 30,000 people must now be employed by the government to monitor and censor the internet. Even with this effort, an estimated 30 percent of controversial messages still get through.

Economic disengagement will not work with China. China is too strategically and economically important to the world.

The U.S. policy of economic engagement and the work of America's internet companies are helping to build the foundations of democratic change in China. But the road is a long one and compromises by American businesses, to maintain their influence in China, are tolerable when viewed within this timeline.

Economic Disengagement Is Not the Answer

Economic sanctions and similar punitive policies have a historically poor track record. According to an American Association for World Health study, "45 years of sanctions have 'dramatically harmed the health and nutrition of large numbers of ordinary Cuban citizens'" without achieving political liberalization. Sanctions on Iran, Iraq, and Burma have produced similar results.

South African sanctions, a success story, show that effective sanctions must pressure democratic governments and must be applied multilaterally by major nations and organizations. China is not democratic; and U.S. disengagement will not be paralleled in other countries. In 2004, China received more than $60 billion in foreign direct investment (FDI)—[Former] French President Jacques Chirac has said France and China should strengthen bilateral economic cooperation. Germany and China recently signed a treaty "fostering bilateral economic relations," and German companies have invested more than $10 billion in China. China is Japan's second-largest trading partner and Japanese FDI is more than $67 billion.

Economic disengagement will not work with China. China is too strategically and economically important to the world. Any U.S. withdrawal would be filled by others and would only result in diminished influence in China and a damaged U.S. economy.

Steps to Improve Social and Political Conditions in China

The ability of American businesses to remain actively involved in Chinese development will ensure that the social conditions necessary for political reform are being developed. But there is more that the U.S. can do to promote these conditions.

To help shift the balance of power away from the political elite, as Huber and Rueschemeyer suggest, the U.S. should work to develop Chinese institutions that enforce the rule of law. These institutions are growing in China. China's World Trade Organization (WTO) membership has imposed laws on its dealings with companies and, as the private sector grows, there is an increased demand to define and protect property. Many social groups are "increasingly resorting to the law to protect their rights or protest perceived injustice" [according to academic M.E. Gallagher]. The Chinese government is promoting these institutions "as a way of both staving off demands for further political liberalization and forcing societal demands into channels under its control," [writes Gallagher,] but the U.S. has an opportunity to influence their development by offering assistance to "China's fledgling legal system," [according to researcher Minxin Pei].

To improve Chinese understanding of democratic societies and to improve U.S. understanding of China's unique situation, the U.S. should work to increase bilateral exchanges between the two nations. In 2004, the United States issued 25,647 student and exchange visitor visas to Chinese nationals, an infinitesimally small percentage of the population. The idea of democracy spreads faster when more people have a vivid experience of it. But increased exchanges should not be limited to students. Minxin Pei, a senior associate at the Carnegie Endowment for International Peace, also recommends "efforts to promote legislative exchanges between Congress and its Chinese counterpart, the National People's Congress; creation of new programs targeting Chinese local legislators; high-level academic exchanges designed to influence elite-level thinking about political reform; technical assistance to village elections; and activities facilitating exchanges between civil society groups." There is a lot of room for the U.S. to enhance the influence of its society on Chinese society.

Lastly, to provide the Chinese people with unfettered access to the internet and to mitigate the consequences of compromises, on the part of America's internet companies with the Chinese government, the U.S. Congress should pass the Global Internet Freedom Act. This bill, introduced by Rep. Chris Cox (R-CA) and Sen. Ron Wyden (D-OR) in 2003, "creates, and authorizes funding for, a new Office of Global Internet Freedom to counter Internet jamming and blocking by repressive regimes." [The act was renamed the Global Online Freedom Act in 2007. As of April 2008, it had not been put to a vote.] Employment of effective countercensorship technologies minimizes the negative impact of doing business in China and helps the Chinese people to become informed enough to press for political reform.

U.S. disengagement from China as a response to its lack of political reform is a bad idea. The conditions for such a strategy to be successful are missing. Continued engagement is a better option. Not only is it beneficial to the U.S. economy, it is having a major impact on Chinese development. Economic development, coupled a stronger rule of law, [with] increased exchange programs, and countercensorship technologies will create the social conditions necessary for China's successful political liberalization.

4

Economic Engagement May Have No Effect on China's Government

James Mann

James Mann is author-in-residence at Johns Hopkins University's School of Advanced International Studies and a former foreign affairs columnist for the Los Angeles Times.

The U.S. government and American businesses may be wrong to believe trade with China will bring democracy to that nation. Instead, the result may be that China remains a one-party state and helps create a world in which political repression becomes widely acceptable. Furthermore, any improvement in the living conditions of Chinese citizens due to economic engagement is limited largely to the urban middle class, who would likely not benefit if China held free elections and thus have an incentive to oppose democracy. The United States must realize that democracy may not be in China's future and reconsider whether free trade is a useful approach to take.

America has been operating with the wrong paradigm for China. Day after day, U.S. officials carry out policies based upon premises about China's future that are at best questionable and at worst downright false.

The mistake lies in the very assumption that political change—and with it, eventually, democracy—is coming to

James Mann, "America's China Fantasy," *American Prospect*, vol. 18, no. 3, March 2007. www.prospect.org. Copyright © 2007 The American Prospect, Inc. All rights reserved. Reproduced with permission from *The American Prospect*, 11 Beacon Street, Suite 1120, Boston, MA 02108.

China, that China's political system is destined for far-reaching liberalization. Yet the [George W.] Bush administration hasn't thought much about what it might mean for the United States and the rest of the world to have a repressive one-party state in China three decades from now. For while China will certainly be a richer and more powerful country in 30 years, it could still be an autocracy of one form or another. Its leadership (the Communist Party, or whatever else it calls itself in the future) may not be willing to tolerate organized political opposition any more than it does today.

That is a prospect with profound implications for the United States and the rest of the world. And it is a prospect that our current paradigm of an inevitably changing China cannot seem to envision.

The notion of a China on the road to political liberalization has taken hold in the United States because it has served certain specific interests within American society. At first, in the late 1970s and the 1980s, this idea benefited the U.S. national-security establishment. At the time, the United States was seeking close cooperation with China against the Soviet Union, so that the Soviet Union would have to worry simultaneously about both countries; the Pentagon wanted to make sure the Soviet Union tied down large numbers of troops along the Sino-Soviet border that might otherwise have been deployed in Europe. Amid the ideological struggles of the Cold War, though, cooperation with China's Communist regime was politically touchy in Washington. And so the notion that China was in the process of opening up its political system helped smooth the way with Congress and the American public.

Trade May Not Lead to Democracy

In the 1990s, after the Soviet collapse, the idea of a politically changing China attracted a new constituency, one even more powerful than the Pentagon: the business community. As trade and investment in China became ever more important, American companies found themselves repeatedly beset with questions about why they were doing business with such a repressive regime. The paradigm of inevitable change offered multinational corporations the answer they needed. Not only was China destined to open up its political system, but trade, the theology held, would be the key that would unlock the door. It would lead to political liberalization and to democracy, with or without the support of the Chinese leadership. Accordingly, no one outside China needs to do anything, or even think much about the subject. Why bother to protest a crackdown or urge China to allow political opposition if you know that democracy, by the inexorable laws of history, is coming anyway?

The trouble is, the entire paradigm may turn out to be wrong.

What should the U.S. strategy be for dealing with China's Leninist regime? If you ask our established political leaders, foreign-policy experts, or sinologists what the United States should do about China, you will undoubtedly get some version or another of this approach. It is called the strategy of "integration."

The United States, the thinking goes, should try to integrate the Chinese leadership into the international community. It should seek to help China gain admission into the world's leading international organizations. According to this logic, the nature of the Chinese regime will change after China becomes a member of international bodies such as the World Trade Organization, which it has now joined. China's Communist Party leadership will gradually behave more like other governments; it will become more open in dealing with the Chinese people and with the rest of the world. Richard Haass, the president of the Council on Foreign Relations, has written of "the existing opportunity to integrate China into a U.S.-led world order."

This strategy of integration dates back to the Clinton administration. In 1994, President Clinton abandoned his attempt to use trade as a lever for improving human rights in China, then needed to divert attention away from this embarrassing reversal. He did not wish to concede that he had just downgraded the cause of human rights in China; instead, he sought a new, positive-sounding description of his policy. "Integration" gradually became the label of choice, invoked by the president and his top advisers in press conference after press conference. Integration became, above all, the justification for unrestricted trade with China. "We believe it's the best way to integrate China further into the family of nations and to secure our interests and our ideals," declared Clinton in one typical speech.

George W. Bush and his advisers, without ever admitting they were doing so, have perpetuated most of the essentials of Clinton's China policy, including the avowed commitment to integration. When Secretary of State Condoleezza Rice gives a speech about China, she sooner or later calls for integrating China into the international community.

Is China now integrating the United States into a new international political order where democracy is no longer favored?

"Integration" has thus become another catchphrase like "engagement," the earlier slogan for America's China policy, which originated somewhat earlier, during the administration of George Bush Senior. With both words, however, the suggestion is the same: that is, with enough engagement, with sufficiently vigorous integration, the United States may succeed in altering the nature of the Chinese regime—although it is not clear exactly how this is supposed to happen. In a way, the American approach is a bit patronizing to China: It sounds as if the United States is a weary, experienced trainer bringing China to a diplomatic version of obedience school.

China Undermines Democracy

The fundamental problem with this strategy of integration is that it raises the obvious question: Who's integrating whom? Is the United States now integrating China into a new international economic order based upon free-market principles? Or is China now integrating the United States into a new international political order where democracy is no longer favored, and where a government's continuing eradication of all organized political opposition is accepted or ignored?

This is not merely a government issue. Private companies—including Internet firms like Yahoo, Google, and Microsoft—often use slogans like "engagement" and "integration" to explain why they have decided to do business in China despite Chinese rules and laws that allow continuing censorship. "I think [the Internet] is contributing to Chinese political engagement," Bill Gates told one business gathering. Yet if Microsoft is altering its rules to accommodate China, once again the question is: Who's changing whom?

Will it have been a success for the U.S. policy of integration if, 30 years from now, the world ends up with a Chinese regime that is still a deeply repressive one-party state but is nevertheless a member of the international community in good standing? If so, that same China will serve as a model for dictators, juntas, and other undemocratic governments throughout the world—and in all likelihood, it will be a leading supporter of these regimes. Pick a dictator anywhere today and you'll likely find that the Chinese regime is supporting him. It has rewarded Robert Mugabe, the thug who rules Zimbabwe, with an honorary professorship, and his regime with economic aid and, reportedly, new surveillance equipment. It has been the principal backer of the military regime in Burma. And when Uzbek President Islam Karimov ordered a murderous crackdown on demonstrators in 2005, China rushed to defend him.

If China maintains its current political system over the next 30 years, then its resolute hostility to democracy will have an impact in places like Egypt, Syria, and Saudi Arabia. A permanently authoritarian China could also undermine Russia's already diminishing commitment to democracy.

Thus, when America's leading officials and CEOs speak so breezily of integrating China into the international community, listeners should ask: If China remains unchanged, what sort of international community will that be? Will it favor the right to dissent? Will it protect freedom of expression? Or will it simply protect free trade and the right to invest?

But wait, say the defenders of America's existing China policy. We believe in democracy, too. There is no real disagreement here on our ultimate goals. This is all just a question of tactics. The strategy of integration (or of engagement) is designed to change China's political system and, over the long term, to end China's one-party state.

These arguments sound in some ways similar to claims made by the Chinese regime itself. Because Chinese Communist Party leaders don't like to acknowledge that they intend to maintain their monopoly on power, they sometimes tell visitors that they, too, believe in democracy, that this is the ultimate goal for China, and that it is all merely a question of timing. These claims are designed for the hopelessly gullible; by its actions, day after day, the regime makes clear its tenacious hostility to the idea of political pluralism in China.

Generally, the U.S. proponents of a strategy of integration are not so cynical. To be sure, a few of them may be antidemocratic; there have always been Americans who admire, even revere, the simplicity and convenience of autocracy. However, other proponents of integration seem to believe quite sincerely that if the United States continues its current approach toward China, Chinese leaders eventually will be willing to abandon the monopoly on political power they have maintained since 1949. Yet these same proponents fail to explain how or why, given the current U.S. strategy, China's political system will change.

The Rule of Law May Have Little Impact

The examples of reforms that they have invoked so far have served to divert attention away from the core issue of China's one-party state. The promotion of village elections has proved to be largely unsuccessful, both because the Chinese leadership can confine this experiment exclusively to the villages and because in the villages themselves, authorities have resorted to a variety of methods, including the use of violence, to forestall democracy.

Nor is there evidence that the American promotion of the rule of law will by itself transform the political system. So long as there is no independent judiciary and China remains a one-party regime in which judges are selected by the Communist Party, promoting the rule of law won't bring about fundamental change. Instead, it simply may lead to a more thoroughly legalized system of repression. Indeed, those lawyers in China who attempt to use the judicial system to challenge the Communist Party or to defend the rights of political dissidents have themselves been subject to persecution, including the loss of their jobs or even time in prison.

The strongest impetus for establishing the rule of law comes from the corporations and investors who are putting their money into China. They need bona fide procedures for resolving financial disputes, just as companies and investors require everywhere else in the world. It is in the interest of the Chinese regime to keep the investment dollars, euros, and yen flowing into the country, and so Chinese officials are willing to establish some judicial procedures for the foreign companies. However, the result could well be a Chinese legal system that offers special protection for foreign investors but not to ordinary Chinese individuals, much less to targets of the regime such as political dissidents or Tibetan activists.

Democracy ... is a threat to the existing political and economic order in China.

And that raises the larger question about America's current strategy of integration: Whom does it benefit? Above all, it enriches the elites in both China and the United States. The strategy is good for the American business community, which gets to trade with China and invest in China, *and* for the new class emerging in Chinese cities—the managers and entrepreneurs, many of them former party cadres or the relatives of cadres—that is getting rich from the booming trade and investment in its country. But it has not been nearly so beneficial for working-class Americans—particularly the tens of thousands who have lost their jobs in the United States as the end result of this "integration" policy.

China's Prosperity Is Limited

The American people were told many years ago that bringing China into the international economic system would help change the Chinese political system. Now, American workers may well wonder whether this argument was merely a cruel hoax. Nor has the strategy of integration been such a blessing for ordinary Chinese. To be sure, China as a whole is more prosperous than it has ever been, but this new prosperity is enjoyed mostly by the urban middle class, not by the country's overworked, underpaid factory laborers or by the hundreds of millions of peasants in the countryside.

Indeed, it is precisely because the regime knows how restive and disenchanted the Chinese people are that it refuses to open up to any form of democracy. The Chinese leaders know that they could be thrown out of office if there were free and open elections. Democracy, or even an organization calling for future democracy, is a threat to the existing political and economic order in China. That is why the regime continues to repress all forms of organized dissent and political opposition. It is also why China's new class of managers and executives, who profit from keeping wages low, support the regime in its ongoing repression.

A few years ago, *New York Times* columnist Nicholas D. Kristof gave voice to one of the most common American misconceptions about China's political future. Reflecting on how China had progressed and where it was headed, Kristof wrote, "[Hard-liners] knew that after the Chinese could watch Eddie Murphy, wear tight pink dresses and struggle over what to order at Starbucks, the revolution was finished. No middle class is content with more choices of coffees than of candidates on a ballot."

Once people are eating at McDonald's or wearing clothes from the Gap, American writers rush to proclaim that these people are becoming like us, and that their political system is therefore becoming like ours. But will the newly enriched, Starbucks-sipping, condo-buying, car-driving denizens of China's largest cities in fact become the vanguard for democracy in China? Or is it possible that China's middle-class elite will either fail to embrace calls for a democratic China or turn out to be a driving force in *opposition* to democracy?

China's emerging urban middle class, after all, is merely a small proportion of the country's overall population—far smaller than its counterparts in Taiwan or South Korea. There are an estimated 800 million to 900 million Chinese peasants—most of them living in rural areas, although 100 million or more are working or trying to find jobs as migrants on the margins of Chinese cities. If China were to have nationwide elections, and if peasants were to vote their own interests, then the urban middle class would lose. The margin would not be close. On an electoral map of China, the biggest cities—Shanghai, Beijing, Tianjin, Guangzhou, and the others—might look something like the small gold stars on the Chinese flag: They would be surrounded by a sea of red. Add together the populations of China's 10 largest cities and you get a total of some 62 million people. That number is larger than the population of France or Britain or Italy. But it is still only about 5 percent of China's overall population of 1.3 billion.

If you are a multinational company trying to sell consumer products, then the rapid rise in spendable income in China's largest cities is of staggering importance. When it comes to any national elections, however, that new Chinese middle class is merely a drop in the bucket. Those in China's urban avant-garde have every reason to fear that they would be outvoted.

China's urban residents have an even greater reason to fear democracy: The Communist Party has not exactly been even-handed in its treatment of urban residents vis-à-vis peasants. On the contrary: Its policies have strongly favored the cities over the countryside. This is why there has been a wave of protests in the countryside, arising out of land seizures, local taxes, disputes over village elections, and similar controversies. It is also why the Chinese regime has been, in recent years, particularly fearful of mass movements that might sweep through the countryside and undermine the Communist Party's control. Looking at Falun Gong, the quasi-religious movement that began to take hold during the 1990s, the Chinese leadership was haunted by a specter from the past: the Taiping Rebellion, which swept out of middle China in the 19th century and shook the Qing Dynasty to its foundations.

What lies behind the Chinese Communist Party's monopoly on power and its continuing repression of dissent? The answer usually offered is the Communist Party itself—that the party and its more than 70 million members are clinging to their own power and privileges. This is certainly part of the answer, but not all of it. As China's economy has thrived in recent years, strong economic and social forces have also emerged in Chinese society that will seek to protect the existing order and their own economic interests. The new middle class in Chinese cities is coming to favor the status quo nearly as much as does the Communist Party itself.

Why do we assume that what follows the Chinese Communist Party's eventual fall will necessarily be political liberalization or democracy? One can envision other possibilities. Suppose, for example, that the party proves over the next decade to be no better at combating the country's endemic corruption than it has been over the past decade. Public revulsion over this corruption reaches the point where the Chinese people take to the streets; leaders find they cannot depend on troops to quell these demonstrations; the Communist Party finally gives way. Even then, would the result be Chinese democracy? Not necessarily. China's urban middle class might choose to align itself with the military and the security apparatus to support some other form of authoritarian regime, arguing that it is necessary to do so in order to keep the economy running.

[Trade] is not a magic political potion for democracy.

The underlying premise of the U.S. integration strategy is that we can put off the question of Chinese democracy. But two or three decades from now, it may be too late. By then, China will be wealthier, and the entrenched interests opposing democracy will probably be much stronger. By then, China will be so thoroughly integrated into the world financial and diplomatic systems that, because of the country's sheer commercial power, there will be no international support for any movement to open up China's political system.

A Better Approach Toward China

What should the United States do to encourage democratic change in China? A detailed list of policies can emerge only after we first rid ourselves of the delusions and the false assumptions upon which our China policy has long been based.

Above all, we have to stop taking it for granted that China is heading inevitably for political liberalization and democracy. President [George W.] Bush has continued to repeat the American mantra about China, every bit as much as did his predecessors. "As China reforms its economy, its leaders are finding that once the door to freedom is opened even a crack, it cannot be closed," Bush declared in one typical speech. Such words convey a heartwarming sense of hopefulness about China, but they do not match the reality of China itself, where doors are regularly opened by more than a crack and then closed again.

America's political and corporate leaders also need to stop spreading the lie that trade will bring an end to China's one-party political system. This fiction has been skillfully employed, over and over again, to help win the support of Congress and the American public for approval of trade with China. Trade is trade; its benefits and costs are in the economic sphere. It is not a magic political potion for democracy, nor has it brought an end to political repression or to the Chinese Communist Party's monopoly on power, and there is not the slightest reason to think it will do so in the future. In fact, it is possible that our trade with China is merely helping the autocratic regime to become richer and more powerful.

America's current China policy amounts to an unstated bargain: We have abandoned any serious attempt to challenge China's one-party state, and in exchange we have gotten the right to unfettered commerce with China.

What we need now, above all, are political leaders who are willing to challenge America's stale logic and phraseology concerning China. We need politicians who will call attention to the fact that America has been carrying out a policy that benefits U.S. and Chinese business interests far more than it helps ordinary working people in either country.

The reexamination should apply to both U.S. political parties and to both poles of the ideological spectrum. On the Democratic left, we need people who will question the assumptions that it is somehow "progressive" to say that democracy doesn't matter or that it will automatically come to China some day. Such views aren't in the least bit progressive, liberal, or enlightened. Rather, they were developed by the Clinton administration to justify policies that would enable Bill Clinton to win corporate support. During the 1990s, there were other views concerning China within the Democratic Party— those of Nancy Pelosi, for example, and George Mitchell, who took strong stands on behalf of human rights in China. The Democrats rejected those alternative approaches a decade ago. They would do well to reexamine them now.

Within the Republican Party, we need political leaders willing to challenge the Business Roundtable mentality that has dominated the party's thinking on China for so long. If Republicans really care about political freedom, then why should they allow U.S. policy toward China to be dominated by corporate interests while the world's most populous country is governed by a single party that permits no political opposition? President Bush has been able to conceal his business-oriented approach to China behind a facade of hawkish rhetoric. Republicans should not allow this to happen again.

Once the United States finally recognizes that China is not moving inevitably toward democracy, we can begin to decide what the right approach should be. On the one hand, it's possible that America may seek new measures to goad the Chinese leadership toward democratic change. America also might want to reconsider its doctrinaire adherence to free trade in dealing with China. On the other hand, it's possible that the American people may decide that there's absolutely nothing that the United States can or should do about a huge, permanently undemocratic, enduringly repressive China. Such an entity, a Chinese autocracy persisting into the mid-21st century, would cause large problems for U.S. policy elsewhere in the world. Nevertheless, after weighing the costs and benefits of trying to push for democracy in China, the United States could opt for a policy of sheer acceptance of the existing order.

The American people are not being given such options now, however, because the choices are not being laid out. American politicians of both parties talk regularly as if liberalization and democracy are on the way in China. But what if China remains an autocracy? At the moment, that possibility seems to be outside our public discourse. We need to change that in order to figure out what we want to do.

It would be heartening if China's leaders proceed along the lines that America's political leaders predict. It would be wonderful if China opens up, either gradually or suddenly, to a new political system in which the country's 1.3 billion people are given a chance to choose their own leaders. While wishing for such an outcome, however, I will not hold my breath.

5

U.S. Economic Policies Should Change to Benefit from China's Growth

David H. McCormick

David H. McCormick is the under secretary for international affairs at the U.S. Department of the Treasury.

China is facing new challenges as its economy grows, including a decline in consumption and wages and strains on the environment and energy supply. American investment can help China continue its growth and build a modern financial sector. One element of investment is increased currency flexibility, which will make prices more stable and encourage employment. Furthermore, the United States must avoid protectionist tactics and focus on long-term gains.

The United States and China are global economic leaders: they have accounted for over 40 percent of total global economic growth in the past five years, and each is an important market for the other. For example, U.S. exports of services to China support some 37,000 jobs in high-paying, high-productivity sectors of the U.S. economy. And imports from China provide U.S. consumers and companies with greater consumer choices and access to more efficient global supply chains. For China, access to the U.S. and international markets—and openness to international investment—has helped

David H. McCormick, "The Great China Challenge: America's G7 Deputy Makes the Case That When China Succeeds, America Succeeds," *The International Economy*, vol. 21, no. 4, fall 2007, pp. 74–77. Copyright © 2007 International Economy Publications, Inc. Reproduced by permission.

to create a world-class export sector and to drive the spectacular rates of economic growth that have turned this country into the global economic leader it is today.

Economic Challenges Facing China

But China's economy has changed fundamentally over the past thirty, and even ten years, and the Chinese now face a set of new and different challenges in sustaining future economic growth. The growth model that has transformed China from a largely homogeneous, agricultural economy into a dynamic, increasingly technologically sophisticated economy has been hugely successful to this point. But some of the policies developed for a far different China are now responsible for the buildup of large and rising imbalances.

China's most senior leaders have clearly identified these imbalances. They include imbalances in growth between rural and urban areas, between the coast and the interior, between economic and social advancement, between reliance on internal and external demand, between rich and poor households, and between economic development and environmental protection.

Based on China's current growth model, these challenges are likely to grow. China's growth model for the past several decades has featured high levels of investment in physical inputs to production, such as plants for producing manufacturing exports, but has done comparatively less to foster innovation, and the development of deep and competitive markets. The current growth model has served China well to this point, but it is now exacerbating some of the challenges in achieving balanced growth.

First, growth has been increasingly energy-intensive and environmentally unfriendly despite Chinese leaders' efforts to strengthen and enforce environmental regulations. Since 2001, the ratio of growth in energy demand to GDP [gross domestic product] growth in China—a good measure of the energy-intensity of growth—has tripled relative to levels of the previous two decades, putting more pressure on energy supply and increasing the environmental damage from growth.

Second, growth has been highly capital-intensive, reducing the rate at which incremental growth creates new employment opportunities for the Chinese people. Capital and labor are substitutes in economic production, and in an environment of cheap money, Chinese firms have had strong incentives to use more capital and less labor despite China's need to provide jobs for many workers who are now seeking to move from the state and agricultural sectors to the private manufacturing and services sectors.

Third, recent growth has gone hand-in-hand with a decline in both consumption as a share of GDP and household income as a share of GDP. National saving has risen to its highest rate since the beginning of market reforms, and the share of wages in GDP has fallen more than 10 percentage points in less than ten years. This is not unrelated to the increasing capital share of economic output, as much of the increase in savings has come from the corporate sector. As a result, the Chinese people are capturing an increasingly smaller share of the benefits of growth.

Necessary Economic Reforms

These features of the current growth model are mutually reinforcing. The capital-intensive nature of China's economic growth has been fueled by high national saving, which has both provided the resources for capital investment and encouraged the use of capital-intensive techniques. The pattern of prices—maintained by an inflexible exchange rate—has encouraged production in export industries, many of which are highly resource-intensive. At the same time, as Chinese production has increasingly targeted foreign consumers, domestic consumption has remained low, and the resulting high saving has been channeled back into investment in export sectors, perpetuating the cycle.

High and increasing national saving—and its counterpart, the slow growth of domestic demand—has led to increasing trade surpluses and made Chinese growth increasingly dependent on external demand.

Developing a modern financial sector is not an easy thing, but investment by foreign firms ... can play an important role in expediting the process.

China's leaders understand these issues well and are right to be turning their attention now, rather than later, to reforms aimed at achieving economic growth that stems more from domestic demand, innovation, and high quality investment. These reforms include efforts to rebuild the social safety net and address the causes of precautionary household saving, efforts to make education less costly and more widely available, efforts to improve environmental safeguards, and efforts to build a more robust services sector.

The development of the financial services sector—including increased access to consumer finance for Chinese households—will be particularly important to ensuring that strong Chinese growth continues. Access to capital is key to ensuring that Chinese entrepreneurs are able to take full advantage of their capacity for innovation. And access to a wider range of higher-yielding savings instruments would provide all Chinese households with the tools they need to build assets more rapidly, allowing for higher consumption and living standards both today and in retirement. Developing a modern financial sector is not an easy thing, but investment by foreign firms— and the advanced risk-management skills and market expertise that comes with it—can play an important role in expediting the process.

The Effects of Exchange Rate Flexibility

While rebalancing growth will require a number of the major structural changes, price measures, including exchange rate adjustment, must also play a role. Flexible prices play a critical function of allocating resources on the basis of accurately-matched costs and benefits, and they fulfill this function with great effectiveness and at very low cost. The exchange rate has become a highly charged issue in U.S.-China economic relations. This is unfortunate, because as many non-official and non-American observers have argued, exchange rate flexibility is extremely important to China. But it is important to understand what increased currency flexibility in China will, and will not, do for the United States and China.

For the United States, what it will not do is significantly reduce the overall U.S. trade deficit, nor will it provide a magic bullet for solving the problems of American industries facing overseas competition. What increased currency flexibility will do is remove a major cause of the perceived unfairness in our bilateral relationship, allowing us to move on to the important long-term challenges the United States and China jointly face.

For China, more currency flexibility will not restrain growth. Nor will it lead to deflation. We have already seen the resilience of China's exporters to currency appreciation, with many enjoying higher profit margins today than they did two years ago. East Asia, South Korea, Indonesia, and Australia have all had currency appreciations far larger than China's, while maintaining strong growth and price stability.

What currency flexibility will do for China is support—and in fact be a necessary component of—a growth strategy that brings higher consumption to Chinese households and more balanced, sustainable growth. This transition will occur through a decrease in the price of imports and the introduction of stronger incentives for Chinese companies to produce for Chinese consumers. What currency reform will also do is provide Chinese policymakers with greater freedom to use monetary policy to maintain price stability and avoid asset bubbles. This is of particular significance given China's recent acceleration of inflation. All of this will lead to growth that is more stable, more China-centered, and more effective in raising the living standards of the Chinese people than China's current growth model now is.

There are many in China who have expressed concern that more rapid currency appreciation will hurt low-income workers in some sectors. To the contrary, by encouraging employment growth in less capital-intensive domestic-oriented industries, exchange rate appreciation will open up new opportunities for low- and unskilled workers. Even more important for the poor is that industries serving domestic consumption demand will create new jobs at a much faster rate. According to a recent study by economist Robert Feenstra from the University of California at Davis, growth in domestic demand has proven three times more effective in generating employment in China than growth in exports.

It is vital that the U.S. and Chinese economies continue to grow strongly and in ways that do not worsen global or domestic imbalances.

Protectionism Is Not the Answer

The U.S. trade deficit and China's trade surplus are outcomes that are not only driven by international economic factors, but also by domestic economic factors. For the United States, our trade deficit can only be reduced through decisive measures to increase both private and public saving—the opposite problem China faces in its efforts to reduce a large trade surplus. To meet this challenge, we are committed to continuing to improve our fiscal outlook, particularly through measures to address the challenge of entitlement spending reform.

The United States must also avoid the siren song of protectionism. We must not sacrifice the long-term gains of openness by pursuing short-term and misguided responses to the challenges presented by global international markets. President [George W.] Bush and U.S. Treasury Secretary Henry Paulson are committed to maintaining America's open trade and investment climate.

It is vital that the U.S. and Chinese economies continue to grow strongly and in ways that do not worsen global or domestic imbalances. Yet in today's dynamic global economy, recipes for past success do not guarantee success in the future. In the end, to ensure vibrant economies that provide prosperity for their peoples, China and the United States need to adapt their policies to the realities of today's globalizing world—and tomorrow's.

Recalls of Products Made in China Are a Serious Problem

Eric S. Lipton and David Barboza

Eric S. Lipton and David Barboza are reporters for the New York Times.

Approximately 75 percent of the toys bought in the United States are made in China. However, these products also make up 60 percent of toy recalls. Reasons for recalls include the use of lead paint and safety hazards such as sharp edges. Because the Consumer Product Safety Commission does not have sufficient staff to inspect all imported toys, it has become the responsibility of the U.S. toy industry and parents to inspect toys.

China manufactured every one of the 24 kinds of toys recalled for safety reasons in the United States so far [in 2007], including the enormously popular Thomas & Friends wooden train sets, a record that is causing alarm among consumer advocates, parents and regulators.

The latest recall, announced [in June 2007], involves 1.5 million Thomas & Friends trains and rail components—about 4 percent of all those sold in the United States over the last two years by RC2 Corporation of Oak Brook, Ill. The toys were coated at a factory in China with lead paint, which can damage brain cells, especially in children.

Just [since May 2007], a ghoulish fake eyeball toy made in China was recalled after it was found to be filled with kero-

Eric S. Lipton and David Barboza, "As More Toys Are Recalled, Trail Ends in China," *New York Times*, June 19, 2007. www.nytimes.com. Reproduced by permission.

sene. Sets of toy drums and a toy bear were also recalled because of lead paint, and an infant wrist rattle was recalled because of a choking hazard.

China [in 2007] is responsible for about 60 percent of all product recalls, compared with 36 percent in 2000.

The Rise in Chinese Recalls

Overall, the number of products made in China that are being recalled in the United States by the federal Consumer Product Safety Commission has doubled in the last five years, driving the total number of recalls in the country to 467 [in 2006], an annual record.

It also means that China [in 2007] is responsible for about 60 percent of all product recalls, compared with 36 percent in 2000.

Much of the rise in China's ranking on the recall list has to do with its corresponding surge as the world's toy chest: toys made in China make up 70 to 80 percent of the toys sold in the country, according to the Toy Industry Association.

Combined with the recent scares in the United States of Chinese-made pet food, and globally of Chinese-made pharmaceuticals and toothpaste, the string of toy recalls is inspiring new demands for stepped-up enforcement of safety by United States regulators and importers, as well as by the government and industry in China.

"These are items that children are supposed to be playing with," said Prescott Carlson, co-founder of a Web site called the Imperfect Parent, which includes a section that tracks recalls of toys and other baby products. "It should be at a point where companies in the United States that are importing these items are held liable."

The toy trains and railroad pieces are made directly for RC2 at plants it oversees in China, presumably giving it some control over the quality and safety of the toys made there. Staci Rubinstein, a spokeswoman for RC2, declined . . . to comment on safety control measures at company plants in China.

The Toy Industry Association, which represents most American toy companies and importers, also declined to comment.

Julie Vallese, a spokeswoman for the Consumer Product Safety Commission, said the agency recognizes that more must be done to prevent the importation of hazardous toys and other products from China. "It is a big concern. And the agency is taking steps to try to address that as quickly as possible," Ms. Vallese said. "Their businesses will suffer if they don't meet safety standards."

Scott J. Wolfson, a second Consumer Product Safety Commission spokesman, would not say how long ago RC2 discovered the problem or when it first reported it to federal authorities.

Insufficient Safety Resources

[Since 2005], the staff of the consumer product commission has been cut by more than 10 percent, leaving fewer regulators to monitor the safety of the growing flood of imports.

Some consumer advocates say that such staff cuts under the Bush administration have made the commission a lax regulator. The commission, for example, acknowledged in a recent budget document that "because of resource limitations," it was planning next year to curtail its efforts aimed at preventing children from drowning in swimming pools and bathtubs.

The toy industry in the United States is largely self-policed. The Consumer Product Safety Commission has safety standards, but it has only about 100 field investigators and compliance personnel nationwide to conduct inspections at ports, warehouses and stores of $22 billion worth of toys and tens of billions of dollars' worth of other consumer products sold in the country each year. "They don't have the staff that they need to try to get ahead of this problem," said Janell Mayo Duncan, senior counsel at the Consumers Union, which publishes *Consumer Reports*. "They need more money and resources to do more checks."

Among the toy recalls, the problem is most acute with low-price, no-brand-name toys that are often sold at dollar stores.

Most recalls are done voluntarily, as was the case with Thomas & Friends, after companies discover problems or receive complaints.

Among the toy recalls, the problem is most acute with low-price, no-brand-name toys that are often sold at dollar stores and other deep discounters, which are manufactured and sent to the United States often without the involvement of major American toy importers. [In 2006], China also was the source of 81 percent of the counterfeit goods seized by Customs officials at ports of entry in the United States—products that typically are not made according to the standards on the labels they are copying.

The Chinese Response

At one of the RC2 factories in Dongguan, China ... [in June 2007], a pair of workers who were paid about $150 a month to spray paint on mostly metal toy trains six days a week said they did not know whether the paint they used contained lead. The factory produces metal toys as well as the wooden toys listed in the Thomas recall.

"We're just doing the painting," says Li Hong, a 22-year-old factory worker who was sitting out in front of the factory dormitories.

Exactly who operates the factories making the Thomas & Friends trains in Dongguan is unclear. While the zone is run by a group of Chinese or Hong Kong suppliers, it also houses an office building that bears the RC2 corporate logo.

China's own government auditing agency reported [in May 2007] that 20 percent of the toys made and sold in China had safety hazards such as small parts that could be swallowed or sharp edges that could cut a child, according to a report in *China Daily*. Officials in China, of course, are fighting back, insisting that its food and other exports are safe and valuable, that new regulations are being put into place and that problem goods account for a tiny portion of all exports.

The Toy Industry Association urges its members to routinely test products they are importing to make sure they comply with federal safety standards, which prohibit, for example, surface paint that contains lead in toys or items that could cause a choking hazard.

Other major retailers or toy industry companies hit by recalls for products made in China this year include Easy-Bake Ovens, made by Hasbro, which could trap children's fingers in the oven and burn them, and Target stores, which the consumer product commission said was importing and selling Anima Bamboo collection games, some of which were coated with lead paint.

The 22 models of the Thomas & Friends toys that are being recalled include some of the most popular items in the line's collection, such as the red James engine and the fire brigade truck. The toy line, based on the children's book and television series, has an almost fanatical following among some families, who own dozens of models, which can cost $6.50 to $70 each.

Keeping Parents Informed

The string of lead paint cases has drawn the most attention from consumer watchdogs and parenting advice columnists.

"Do I have to look at every toy that has paint on it that comes from China as perhaps suspect?" said Mr. Carlson, of Imperfect Parent.

Ms. Duncan, of Consumers Union, urged parents to sign up for the Consumer Product Safety Commission's automated notification system at the commission's Web site (www.cpsc.gov), so they can stay on top of which toys are being recalled.

Ms. Vallese, the spokeswoman for the product safety commission, said the agency's acting chairwoman, Nancy A. Nord, went to China in May [2007] for a meeting with her counterparts there, focusing in particular on toys, lighters, electronics and fireworks.

"Is there a concern that there are more products coming in from China and making sure they live up to the standards we expect?" Ms. Vallese said. "Yes, there is, and we understand our authority and obligation and we will make sure we enforce it."

But parents shopping for toys in New York over the weekend said the whole episode left them uneasy.

"I think it's terrible," said Chris Gunster, 41, while perusing the Thomas & Friends display area in Toys 'R' Us at Times Square with his wife and 4-year-old son, James, a big fan of the toy trains. "Lead paint in this day and age?"

7

U.S. Laws Can Be Partially Blamed for the Recalls of Chinese-Made Products

Marla Felcher

Marla Felcher is a regular contributor to Mother Jones.

A lack of U.S. government oversight is a major reason why unsafe Chinese products have reached America. Republican presidents have gutted the Consumer Product Safety Commission, the agency that is supposed to ensure that unsafe products do not reach the market. In addition to drastic cuts to its budget and staff, the commission has also become beholden to the toy industry, which decreases the likelihood of recalls.

Late one afternoon in October 2006, Carolyn and Ghassan Daher took their five-year-old son Brayden to a party near Seattle. Kids got goody bags filled with toys and candy; a favorite were the yo-yo water balls, liquid-filled spheres attached to long, stretchy cords. Brayden and his friends hit the kiddie dance floor, swinging the balls over their heads like lassos. Suddenly Brayden came running to his mother, clutching his neck. "His eyes were watering and bloodshot, and I couldn't see anything because the string was clear," Carolyn recalls. "I couldn't see it was around his neck. The ball was pulling down—it was like a rock with flashing colors." After what seemed like an eternity, she was finally able to break the cord. Brayden suffered no permanent injuries.

Marla Felcher, "You're Not the Regulator of Me: How the Bush Administration Made America Safe for Dangerous Toys," *Mother Jones*, November/December 2007. Copyright © 2007 Foundation for National Progress. Reproduced by permission.

But Carolyn was shaken, and when she got home she searched the Internet for information on yo-yo balls. She found that (like most toys in the United States) they are typically imported from China or Taiwan, and that (also like most toys) they have never been tested for safety by the U.S. government. She read about Lisa Lipin, an Illinois mother whose son had nearly been strangled by a yo-yo ball in July 2003. Lipin begged the federal Consumer Product Safety Commission (CPSC) to follow the lead of France, Canada, the United Kingdom, and Australia, and ban the balls. "But they just wanted me to go away," she says. In September of that year, despite close to 200 near-deadly incidents, the CPSC stated that the balls posed "a low risk of strangulation." The agency's chairman, Harold "Hal" Stratton, even told *Good Morning America* that he'd forbidden his own children from playing with the balls—but would not take them off the market. By late 2006, the agency had reports on 416 incidents involving yo-yo balls; 290 of them were classified as strangulation/suffocation.

Gutted Safety Regulations

Ever since Illinois-based RC2 Corp. recalled 1.5 million Thomas the Tank Engine trains in June [2007] after they were found to be coated in lead paint, the headlines have been full of reports on the dangers of Chinese imports—lead paint on Dora the Explorer and Sesame Street toys, Barbies with small magnets that came loose, Playskool sippy cups whose spouts broke off, causing toddlers to choke. Most of the stories have focused on the lack of manufacturer oversight in China. But the root of the problem is closer to home: The CPSC, created to prevent hazardous products from winding up in American homes, has been gutted by decades of manufacturer lobbying and White House interference—and the Bush administration has finally paralyzed it to the point that it can barely function.

"What's going on there is not benign neglect," says Ann Brown, CPSC chairman under President Clinton. "It's the systematic dismantling of the agency."

THE CPSC was created in 1972 with a broad range of powers. It could impose mandatory safety standards, ban or recall products found to be unsafe and dangerous, and levy fines on companies that hid safety information. Its job was to keep tabs on more than 15,000 types of consumer goods— just about everything you'd find in a Wal-Mart except food and drugs. By 1979, it had a budget of $44 million and a staff of nearly 900, whose investigations resulted in 545 recalls that year alone.

The Destruction of the CPSC

Then came the Reagan administration. Within months of taking office, Reagan convinced Congress to pass legislation that crippled the commission: Before it could impose mandatory standards on any product, it had to wait for industry to write its own standards, and then prove that they had failed. Recalls plummeted to fewer than 200 a year, and by 1988 the commission's budget was down 22 percent and its staff had been cut almost in half.

Product-related deaths were up from 22,000 in 1998 to 27,000 [in 2006].

But it was under Hal Stratton, [President] George W. Bush's commission chairman (and former New Mexico attorney general, as well as Lawyers for Bush cochair), that the commission turned from paper tiger to industry lapdog. Stratton cut back on investigations while taking full advantage of the perks of his office—he turned the agency into "a little travel bureau," according to a longtime staffer. When a coalition of doctors and safety advocates asked him to look into the problem of adult-sized all-terrain vehicles marketed to kids, Stratton said he'd do a study. Three years (and more than 400 ATV-related deaths of kids under 16) later, he released the results of fact-finding trips to West Virginia, New Mexico, and Alaska, where he'd met with safety advocates as well as various ATV enthusiast groups. The upshot: a proposal to let kids ride even bigger, more powerful ATVs.

Stratton's departure in 2006 left the agency with a grim record—product-related deaths were up from 22,000 in 1998 to 27,000—and only two commissioners, one from each side of the aisle. Lacking a quorum, much of the commission's work came to a halt. After waiting more than seven months to pick a new chairman, President Bush nominated a senior lobbyist for the very industry the commission regulates: Michael Baroody, of the National Association of Manufacturers. In May [2007], Bush withdrew the nomination after it was disclosed that the association planned to give Baroody a $150,000 severance package when he took his new job. That left the CPSC's Republican commissioner, Nancy Nord—the former director of consumer affairs at the U.S. Chamber of Commerce—in place as acting chairman; she had earlier shown her bona fides by turning down Senate Democrats who wanted to increase the commission's budget. "I'm not trying to fight with you," Senator Mark Pryor (D-Ark.) exasperatedly told her during hearings [in spring 2007]. "I'm trying to get you more money!"

The Magnetix Example

Shortly thereafter, the *Chicago Tribune* reported on a Seattle toddler who had died on Thanksgiving Day, 2005, after swallowing tiny magnets that had spilled from a broken Magnetix building set. The commission had been warned about the hazard of magnetic toys years earlier and failed to act: Just six months before the toddler's death, an Indiana preschool teacher had called to report that one of her students had nearly died when the Magnetix bits he swallowed perforated his bowels.

It wasn't until the following year that CPSC finally recalled the Magnetix sets; its press release reassured consumers that only old sets were problematic, when in fact the hazardous sets were still being sold (and stayed on shelves for another year). This past April [2007] the commission—having now received reports of 29 Magnetix-related injuries, all but one of which had required surgery—expanded the recall to include 4 million more units. (The recall press release, negotiated with the company's lawyers, was so vague, the CPSC had to issue a separate fact sheet later to tell parents which sets were safe to buy and which were not.) Asked by Illinois lawmakers what she planned to do about all this, Nord said her agency needed more money after all.

Nord was called back to Capitol Hill this summer during the Chinese toy recalls. "What we have here is an agency in distress," Senator Pryor told the press. By September [2007], even the toy industry was pleading for new government standards to help reassure jittery consumers (and, quite possibly, preempt lawsuits). "CPSC got caught with their pants down about China," says former commissioner Ann Brown. "Companies know the agency is toothless, so there's no reason for them to worry about the products that they bring into the country."

8

The Chinese Government Exploits Workers Who Make Products for the U.S.

Harry Wu

Harry Wu is a human rights activist who spent nineteen years in a Chinese labor camp.

Companies in China violate international labor standards by forcing prisoners to work in factories without pay, often manufacturing toys. Prisoners work for as long as eighteen hours each day and are tortured or beaten if they protest their conditions. In addition, free workers often labor in sweatshops and are forbidden from joining independent trade unions. The oppressive conditions of Chinese factories helps explain why harmful toys have been exported to the United States, because the Chinese government condones low standards.

Good morning, I would first like to thank the Senate Commerce Subcommittee on Interstate Commerce and Trade and especially Chairman [Byron] Dorgan and his staff for inviting me here today. This issue is extremely timely in light of recent toy recalls, and I am pleased that the United States Senate is concerned about labor conditions in China's toy industry.

I have been asked to focus on the Chinese labor system and the working conditions in toy factories in China. For many years human rights organizations have raised awareness

Harry Wu, *The Chinese Labor System and the Toy Industry*, Hearing Before the Senate Commerce Subcommittee on Interstate Commerce and Trade on Sweatshop Practices in the Chinese Toy Industry, October 25, 2007.

about the atrocious conditions in Chinese sweatshops where workers make most of the clothes we are wearing right now, and most of the toys our children play with. Today my testimony will confirm that Chinese and foreign-owned companies operating in China consistently violate international labor standards in the toy industry and the Chinese Communist Party (CCP) ignores these violations in order to maintain economic growth and foreign investment. The Chinese government placates the international community by agreeing to promote labor rights in multilateral meetings while continuing to allow the abuse of its workers at home.

First, I will cover a subject less discussed in the international arena—forced labor. I will begin with early CCP theories on forcing prisoners to work, and will provide current examples of forced labor being used in the toy industry specifically. Next, I will discuss China's so-called national trade union, the All China Federation of Trade Unions (ACFTU), and its role as one of the Party's many tools to repress its people. I will conclude with what actions the U.S. government and American companies should take.

My knowledge of this subject originates from my 19 years in China's prison camps where I was forced to labor, and from my subsequent work as a human rights activist. I am the founder and the executive director of the Laogai Research Foundation, which began in 1992 for the purpose of researching and raising awareness about China's vast system of prison camps, called the "Laogai," and other human rights abuses in China.

Forced Labor Is Common in China

The Chinese word "laogai," meaning "reform through labor," refers to a system of forced labor camps that spans China's entire territory. Since the inception of the Chinese Communist Party in 1949 the Chinese government's ideology has been to use its people to fulfill its political and economic goals. As a result humans are viewed as expendable commodities. Mao Zedong immediately recognized prisoners as a huge source of manpower, and in 1951 amended the "Resolution of the Third National Public Security Conference" to support this idea:

> The large number of people who are serving their sentences is an enormous source of labor. In order to reform them, in order to solve the problems of the prisons, in order that these sentenced counterrevolutionaries will not just sit there and be fed for nothing, we should begin to organize our Laogai work. In the areas where this work already exists, it should be expanded.

During the 1950s and 60s Laogai inmates were the primary labor force for massive state-run reconstruction projects such as irrigation, mining, and dam projects that would have been impossible to undertake with regular workers. As China's economy developed and it shifted from agriculture to manufacturing, so did the type of work that prisoners were forced to endure. During Deng Xiaoping's reform era the goal for economic development drove the country to open to foreign investment and the importance of forced labor increased. In the 1988 "Criminal Reform Handbook," Deng reiterated that one of the three major functions of the Laogai facilities was to organize "criminals in labor and production, thus creating wealth for society." This amount of profit cannot be underestimated because prisoners are not compensated for their work.

In our foundation's most recent biannual handbook (*Laogai Handbook 2005–2006*) we identified more than 1,100 labor camps by name and location (693 prisons and 352 re-education labor camps). According to our research, there are eleven prisons that produce toys for domestic and international markets in provinces across China and there are likely many more.

These provinces include Beijing, Shanghai, Gansu, Hunan, Hubei, Zhejiang, Shandong, Liaoning, and Henan. In the No. 2 reeducation through labor camp in Shandong province, female prisoners, many of whom are imprisoned for political reasons, are forced to work without pay on handicrafts and toys for international export. Former prisoners from the camp have described some of their tasks to include applying artificial eyelashes and hair to dolls. At the Shiliping reeducation thorough labor camp in Zhejiang province, where profits equal about 80 million yuan or almost 11 million U.S. dollars, inmates produce wool sweaters, leather products, and toys for international export. Hunan province's Chishan Prison forces its inmates to make toys for export to South Korea. At a juvenile detention facility in Shanghai, youths are forced to produce toys, clothes, and other products.

In June 2004, Li Ying a former political prisoner held for two years at the Shanghai Women's reeducation through labor facility talked about the toys she was forced to produce—dolls that were eventually sold in Italy. She asserted that she and her fellow inmates on "Team No. 3" made these dolls from June 2002–May 2003 laboring from 7 a.m. until 11 p.m., and sometimes even until 1 a.m. The prisoners were required to fulfill a quota of 120 dolls per day without pay in horrible working conditions.

The U.S. State Department's annual human rights report from 2006 confirms that "prison labor" is common in China. The report states that throughout last year "prisoners worked in facilities directly connected with penal institutions; in other cases they were contracted to nonprison enterprises. . . . Facilities and their management profited from inmate labor." This fact that companies are using forced labor makes it very likely that some of the toy are entering the United States.

Difficult to Stop the Use of Forced Labor

Unfortunately, the Memorandum of Understanding on Prison Labor signed between the United States and China in the United States has proven to be completely ineffective in stopping the trade in forced labor products. Our own efforts to gather specific evidence are hampered significantly by the fact that China has deemed much information about these camps to be "state secrets." They severely punish anyone who reveals it. While we have revealed much information about the Laogai over the years, we have also contributed to simply forcing the trade to go further underground. The Chinese systematically use legitimate trading companies unconnected to the Laogai to sell the products abroad.

A recent civil case involving the importation of forced-labor-made coffee mugs was brought by a U.S. company in Ohio. Detailed evidence of the production link to Luzhong Prison was presented. Unfortunately, the bringing of such cases is extremely rare, not because forced labor is rare, but rather because it is dangerous and difficult to gather the information in the first place.

Of course, the overwhelming majority of toys made in China are produced in private factories, most of which are foreign-owned. Many of these can and have been defined as "sweatshops" by NGOs [nongovernmental organizations], unions, and journalists in literally hundreds of reports over the past decade.

Forced labor and sweatshop conditions in the toy industry . . . are perpetuated by the Chinese government.

The State Department's investigation also reported the sweatshop conditions that exist in factories, including those that make toys:

> In July more than 1,000 workers at a plastic toy factory in Dongguan, Guangdong province, rioted over allegations of inadequate pay and working conditions, particularly excessive overtime, and protesters clashed with police and company security. Dozens of workers were detained after the two-day protest.

In September [2007,] the Hong Kong labor rights organization, Students and Scholars Against Corporate Misbehaviour, exposed the conditions at a factory in China making toys for Disney. Workers at Haowei Toys in southern China said they were forced to labor for 15 hours a day for 28 days a month during peak seasons using dangerous toxic chemicals.

The labor conditions in prisons and sweatshops are clearly different, but in all too many cases only by degree. If prisoners attempt to defend their rights they are quickly stifled by beatings or even torture. If workers do, they are either fired or arrested. Prisoners labor without remuneration, and many factory workers are denied the pay that is due them for the hours they work. Forced labor and sweatshop conditions in the toy industry like nearly every other industry are perpetuated by the Chinese government because economic profit and GDP [gross domestic product] growth are the CCP's number-one priority. China still refuses to ratify the International Labor Organization's [ILO] convention against forced labor claiming it has a useful purpose in its reeducation camps. The government also will not ratify any United Nations or ILO conventions that allow workers to create and join independent unions and collectively bargain.

[In October 2007] the *Salt Lake Tribune* ran a series of investigative reports on working conditions in Guangdong province by reporter Loretta Tofani entitled "American Imports, Chinese Deaths." It represents a 14-month effort and was sponsored by the Pulitzer Center for Crisis Reporting. With your permission I am attaching it to my testimony for the record. While it does not deal specifically with the toy industry, it is the most current expose of the tragic nature of work in southern China, the very same region where a majority of toys are produced for export to the United States.

No True Unions Are Allowed

The Chinese government outlaws all independent trade unions, forcing workers to join the state-sponsored All China

Federation of Trade Unions (ACFTU). This organization, run by the CCP, with over 170 million members, is used to control union activities and workers. The ultimate goal of the ACFTU is to "uphold ... the leadership of the Communist Party" and to quash any grassroots union movements.

The government's most recent tactic is to co-opt foreign companies into allowing their employees to join the ACFTU under the auspices of protecting the workers. In 2006 Wal-Mart—a company that does not allow its employees to unionize in any other country—finally capitulated to ACFTU demands and currently 77 out of 84 of its stores in China have union branches. This tactic has two motives for the government as its economy shifts to privately owned enterprises. First dues paid by companies with ACFTU branches help offset the losses from the diminishing state-owned sector, and second, the CCP can better monitor and control its private-sector workers.

There is no evidence that Wal-Mart workers are allowed to bargain their own contracts with the company. And, unfortunately, some in the American labor movement have seen fit to ignore the reality that the ACFTU is CCP controlled and an oppressor of workers rather than their advocates and have granted them a legitimacy they don't deserve by meeting and working with them as equals.

The U.S. government has an obligation to ensure that forced labor products and tainted goods do not enter our borders.

Sadly, workers who attempt to organize independent unions are quickly dealt with, usually by arrest and sentencing to serve terms in the Laogai and could end up making the products we are discussing here today.

The U.S. Must Take Responsibility

The labor abuses in the toy industry prove that, despite its rhetoric, China has not progressed in human rights nor does it respect international labor standards. The high number of recalled toys made in China [in 2007] alone should be a sufficient warning for U.S. companies and consumers. The Chinese government continues to use forced labor to make goods, condones sweatshop conditions in its factories, and refuses to allow workers to create independent unions—is it really any wonder that low-quality, harmful toys are being exported to the U.S. and into the hands of our children? The toy industry in China is a vivid example that disproves the commonly mentioned notion that economic development and/or capitalism will bring democratic change to China. In contrast, more and more U.S. companies are bending to the government's demands making the totalitarian regime even stronger.

The U.S. government has an obligation to ensure that forced labor products and tainted goods do not enter our borders. American companies must take responsibility for the Chinese factories that produce their goods. They must perform more frequent inspections and audits and should not allow phony unions to be set up in their factories and workplaces. Profit is the only factor that has the potential to affect China's behavior. Workers' rights in China will not improve until foreign businesses and governments collectively decide to press China to stop using prison and sweatshop labor and to allow their workers to independently organize.

9

The United States Should Improve Working Conditions in China

James P. Hoffa

James P. Hoffa is the president of the Teamsters, a union that represents 1.4 million employees in the transportation, freight, and related industries.

The U.S. government must change practices that have allowed China to exploit its workers. Chinese workers labor under harsh conditions; however, efforts in China to strengthen their rights have been stymied by American businesses, which want goods produced cheaply without extensive regulations. The U.S. government must increase its oversight of goods imported from China and ensure that trade with that nation is fair and not focused solely on costs.

While walking along a Detroit sidewalk [in September 2007,] a friend's 6-year-old son picked up a small, unremarkable golden locket. He chipped away dirt clumps before reading, "Made in China."

He offered me the locket. I told him I didn't see the words. "Where do you see that?" I asked. He grinned, then exploded with laughter—he was fooling me.

Like the best jokes, it contained a nugget of truth. My friend's son had been reading for only a year or two, but he'd come across "made in China" enough to know that the phrase is on countless items. The phrase has become a part of American life.

James P. Hoffa, "Improve Safety for U.S. and China," *Detroit News*, October 12, 2007. Reproduced with permission of *The Detroit News*.

A String of Recalls

Lately, a steady pulse of negative news about poisoned pet food and toothpaste and abysmal working conditions in China has made more of us wary of the phrase. [In October 2007,] the Boy Scouts recalled more than a million badges tainted with lead paint and the Consumer Product Safety Commission recalled another 550,000 products.

Since August [2007], more than 21 million Chinese-made products—including toys from Dora the Explorer, Thomas & Friends and Baby Einstein lines—have been recalled. Three children have been killed in defective playpens, and pets have been poisoned from tainted food. Factor in rampant environmental problems and, increasingly, we're seeking products made anywhere but China.

Horrible Working Conditions Are a Problem in China

Misplaced trade priorities are at the heart of these problems. As corporations have outsourced American manufacturing jobs, our government has sold short the system that protects against unsafe products, allowing workers to be exploited in ruthless pursuit of low-cost cheap goods. We must drastically improve this dangerous arrangement.

In August [2007], China Labor Watch, a U.S.-based workers' rights group, issued a report detailing labor violations and brutal conditions.

"Wages are low, benefits are nonexistent, work environments are dangerous and living conditions are humiliating," the report said of its investigation into plants that make toys for multinational companies.

Two-thirds of China's power comes from coal, and it comes at a steep price. The Chinese government reported more than 4,700 deaths related to coal mining—13 a day, on average—[in 2006], while independent groups estimate 20,000 deaths.

Working conditions in China need to be improved. Norms for working standards worldwide are being set in China.

Change is happening in China, although not easily. In response to mass protests by workers, the Chinese government drafted a law strengthening the workers' union. The law would require employers to enter into contracts with employees, allow workers to change jobs and oblige companies to bargain over health and safety issues. However, U.S. corporations objected, saying they would make it harder to do business.

By allowing goods to be produced in a shallowly regulated China rather than in the much safer United States, we're seeing our safety standards are lowered.

My visit to China convinced me that China is not building a middle class capable of sustaining economic growth. In fact, it created a situation that allows corporations to exploit poorly paid workers in often unsafe conditions. It's time that companies respect workers' rights here and in China.

America Must Improve Labor and Safety Standards

Here at home, the Bush administration has relaxed the regulatory system that protects workers. By allowing goods to be produced in a shallowly regulated China rather than in the much safer United States, we're seeing our safety standards are lowered.

Simultaneously, the Bush administration has cut our capacity to inspect imports. The *New York Times* reports that the Consumer Product Safety Commission "has one lone toy tester, at an outdated lab in Maryland, for the whole country." And while we are importing four times more food from China than we did in 1996, our Food and Drug Administration inspects less than 1 percent of imports. What sort of oversight is that?

Trade should be fair, to benefit our citizens and our trading partners. We must lift labor standards in the United States and around the world.

10

The U.S. Needs a New Way to Address China's Human Rights Violations

Ying Ma

Ying Ma, a former National Research Initiative fellow at the American Enterprise Institute, is a contributor to several magazines, including Weekly Standard *and* Policy Review.

Trade with China has failed to improve human rights in that country. Chinese citizens have made efforts to expose the actions of their government, but China has responded through tactics such as imprisonment and bribery. American politicians who want to better the lives of the Chinese need to recognize that the current approach of economic engagement may not be the solution and start asking tougher questions about U.S. policies.

While Chinese President Hu Jintao prepares to face the White House [in April 2008] on issues ranging from the bilateral trade deficit to China's role in resolving the North Korean and Iranian nuclear crises, Representative Chris Smith (R-NJ) is planning to slam the Chinese regime for its political repression.

The House Subcommittee on Africa, Global Human Rights and International Operations, which Smith chairs, will hold a hearing . . . to condemn the Chinese government for its poli-

cies of religious persecution, forced abortions, Internet censorship, and human organ harvesting.

Unfortunately, few besides Smith's witnesses and the usual human rights activists will care. These days, a tinge of sadness pervades most congressional hearings and resolutions on the important subject of human rights in China. Simply put, China is not listening.

Bilateral trade has failed to make China a more humane place as trade proponents had promised.

It wasn't always this way, and it doesn't have to be this way. Throughout the 1990s, Congress made China's human rights record a crucial consideration in every annual review of China's trade status. But when Congress granted permanent normal trade relations (PNTR) to China in 2000, Washington lost its most potent leverage against Beijing on the issue of human rights.

Trade Has Not Improved Human Rights in China

Having voted against trade with China, many of the most vocal congressional crusaders for human rights in China have viewed every revelation of continued or new human rights violations in China as an opportunity to denounce the approval of PNTR. When revelations surfaced in February [2006] that American companies had acquiesced to Chinese pressure for online censorship, congressmen such as Chris Smith, Dana Rohrabacher and Tom Lantos—all opponents of PNTR—pointed out that bilateral trade has failed to make China a more humane place as trade proponents had promised.

Still, this style of China bashing is no longer sufficient for addressing the shortcomings of Chinese society or the failures of U.S.-China policy. Other members of Congress, having decided to delink the issue of human rights from bilateral trade between the United States and China, show no interest in rehashing that debate again. Legislation introduced by Rep.

Smith to deter and penalize American businesses that collaborate with the Chinese government's internet censorship campaign now languishes in the House.

Within China, the regime continues to resist political liberalization, but it faces intensified opposition from numerous segments of the Chinese population. In recent years, peasants have rioted against land seizures; environmental NGOs [nongovernmental organizations] have drawn attention to toxic drinking water and massive air pollution; Internet users have helped expose government cover-ups like the breakout of the SARS crisis in 2003; lawyers have sued state-owned enterprises on behalf [of] injured or unpaid workers; and public intellectuals continue to decry the regime's complicity in the daily suffering of its citizens.

The Chinese regime has responded to this bourgeoning political opposition with a multi-faceted approach: paying off some while jailing others; restricting the activities of some while cracking down wholesale on others. Meanwhile, it is indoctrinating the public with the idea that continued economic growth requires a measure of stability that only the Communist party can provide.

Will bottom-up pressures from Chinese society force the regime to adopt meaningful political change? Or will the regime merely become more adept and sophisticated in managing popular discontent? No one knows for sure.

Ways the U.S. Can Encourage Political Liberalization

Yet those in Congress dedicated to improving human rights in China, like Rep. Smith, show little inclination to recognize such pressing challenges. They bash the Communist colossus, which is probably cathartic. They press for the release of jailed Chinese dissidents, which continues to be necessary. But they could also do a great deal more to explore ways to support and harness numerous strands of dissent and discontent in China.

First, they ought to ask some tough questions about what the United States can and should do to promote political liberalization in China. Has rule of law assistance to China in fact encouraged the rule of law, or will it merely improve the regime's ability to rule by law? Should the United States massively increase funding for NGOs in China, or will that only draw government ire to Chinese activists? Is it enough to increase funding for media like Voice of America and Radio Free Asia to broadcast into China, or must the United States also worry that its message of freedom is diluted by Chinese nationalism?

Changing the complex China that has emerged under Sino-American economic engagement will require more complex solutions.

As the recent controversy surrounding Cisco, Google, Microsoft and Yahoo! shows, American companies are not human rights watchdogs and are in no position to ask such questions. Similarly, numerous China scholars and congressional members are so enamored with China that they believe any program of dialogue and exchange to be useful, as if dialogue were the end rather than the means. Those congressional critics who have not been afraid to bash China could fill this void.

They could continue to wish that America is not trading with China, or they could recognize that changing the complex China that has emerged under Sino-American economic engagement will require more complex solutions. If they choose the latter, congressional action on human rights in China may finally reemerge from irrelevance with the respect that it deserves.

11

American Companies Should Not Support China's Free Speech Restrictions

Dennis Behreandt

Dennis Behreandt is a contributor to the New American *and the Web editor for the John Birch Society.*

Censorship is prevalent in China, and Chinese citizens who post critical views of the government in online forums are often arrested and placed in labor and reeducation camps. American Internet companies such as Yahoo! and Google have supported censorship by creating China-specific search engines that do not show results banned by the government and by monitoring the communication of Chinese users. These actions are troubling because they suggest that Internet companies do not support free-speech principles and are willing to betray ordinary people in exchange for profits.

For Wang Xiaoning, a political activist in Communist China, the fateful knock at the door came on September 1, 2002—an otherwise peaceful Sunday morning. According to the account provided by Luke O'Brien of *Wired News*, the phone rang that morning while Wang was working at his computer in the Beijing duplex he shared with his wife, Yu Ling, and their son. When Wang answered the phone, a voice on the other side asked simply: "Are you home?" When Wang

Dennis Behreandt, "Internet Crackdown: To Do Business in China, American Companies Have to Play by Beijing's Rules, Even If Doing So Puts Innocent People in Jail," *New American*, vol. 23, no. 11, May 28, 2007, pp. 22–26. Copyright © 2007 American Opinion Publishing Incorporated. Reproduced by permission.

answered, "Yes," the line went dead. Moments later, at least 10 agents of the communist state burst through his door in a violent raid. Confiscating his computer equipment, computer discs, written notes, manuscripts, and address books, they took Wang into custody and left.

On their way out they gave an official notice to the shocked and frightened Yu Ling: "Keep quiet." Since then, Yu Ling hasn't seen her husband except for one half-hour-long prison visit per month. His crime? Calling for political reform of China's single-party communist political system.

Wang Xiaoning's case is just one among thousands—if not millions—of cases in which political dissidents have been jailed in China, thrust into the communist state's repressive labor and reeducation camps. But Wang's case, like a handful of others, is different from most. Like millions, he is the victim of the communist oligarchy in Beijing, a totalitarian despotism that recognizes no rights and that rules with an iron fist. But unlike the millions of other unfortunates that fall afoul of China's state security apparatus, Wang's ticket to the regime's torture and reeducation camps was provided by an American company—pioneering Internet firm Yahoo! Inc.

For . . . dissidents in Communist China, posting political opinions online calling for reform is a dangerous occupation.

Now, in what some are calling a landmark case, Yu Ling, with the assistance of the World Organization for Human Rights USA, has filed a lawsuit on behalf of herself and her husband against Yahoo! in the U.S. District Court for the Northern District of California in San Francisco.

Dangerous Postings

From 2000 until his arrest in 2002, Wang, who has heroically campaigned for a free China for decades, worked as editor of the electronic journals *Free Forum of Political Reform* and *Commentaries on Current Political Affairs*. Both journals carried articles by Wang and others calling for a variety of reforms in China's political system, including the legalization of opposition political parties. While working as editor, Wang also wrote other articles on similar subjects and posted them for a time to a Yahoo! user group identified as "aaabbbccc." In his writings Wang lamented, "China is still an authoritarian dictatorship," and he reminded his readers that in China to this day "workers and peasants have been suppressed into the lowest level of society. Tens of millions of workers are unemployed and many workers are cruelly exploited and oppressed" and have "no protection for their most basic rights."

For Wang, as for other dissidents in Communist China, posting political opinions online calling for reform is a dangerous occupation. According to the OpenNet Initiative, an organization that investigates "state filtration and surveillance practices" online, "China's Internet filtering regime is the most sophisticated effort of its kind in the world," making it next to impossible for dissidents to freely publish their views without, eventually, getting caught. Though Wang was seemingly able to remain somewhat anonymous for a time, the censors were soon on to him.

According to the complaint filed by Yu Ling, "In 2001, administrators noticed the political content of Wang's writings and blocked him from sending messages to the 'aaabbbccc' Yahoo! Group." Not deterred, Wang continued writing, anonymously sending his articles on the need for political reform and freedom in China to a select list of e-mail addresses.

In this he should have been safe. After all, he was e-mailing anonymously using his Yahoo! affiliated account. Chinese authorities should have had no way to track him down through the Yahoo! system, operated as it was by an American company. But unbeknownst to Wang and his family, as a condition of doing business in China, Yahoo! had agreed to play by Beijing's rules.

Helping China Censor Its Citizens

According to the complaint, "In or around the Spring of 2002, Yahoo! Inc. signed an official, voluntary agreement that had the effect of directly involving Yahoo! in the censoring and monitoring of on-line content and communication by its Chinese users. This agreement was in the form of the Internet Society of China's 'Public Pledge on Self-Discipline for the Chinese Internet Industry.'" Under the terms of the pledge, portions of which were published online by *PC World* in 2002, Yahoo! agreed to "monitor the information publicized by users on Web sites according to [Chinese] law and remove the harmful information promptly." In another part of the pledge, Yahoo! agreed to "inspect and monitor the information on [Chinese] domestic and foreign Web sites that have been accessed and refuse access to those Web sites that disseminate harmful information in order to protect the Internet users of China from the adverse influence of the harmful information."

In other words, Yahoo! agreed to help Beijing censor the Internet. But that was not all Yahoo! agreed to do. According to the complaint in the Wang Xiaoning case, the Internet Society of China maintains that, under its pledge, Internet service providers like Yahoo! are also required "to report any offending online expression or communication to PRC [People's Republic of China] authorities." That meant turning over the identities of anonymous online political dissidents to Beijing's Internet gestapo. And that led to Wang's arrest. According to the complaint against Yahoo!, "Yahoo! HK provided identifying information to police, linking Wang Xiaoning to his anonymous e-mails and other pro-democracy Internet communications." He is now serving a 10-year sentence simply for calling for the same basic and intrinsic freedoms enjoyed by Yahoo!'s American business execs.

For its part, Yahoo! says it is just obeying the law and that it has no idea why the Chinese government requests user information or how that information is used once it's turned over to authorities. Compliance, Yahoo! says, is just a condition of business in China, just as it is in other nations—the United States included.

U.S. Internet companies doing business in China have agreed to play ball with Beijing.

In testimony to the Congressional Subcommittees on Africa, Global Human Rights and Asia and the Pacific on February 15, 2006, Michael Callahan, a senior vice president for Yahoo!, addressed the challenges the company faces in complying with Chinese law. "When we receive a demand from law enforcement authorized under the law of the country in which we operate, we must comply," Callahan said in remarks related to the jailing of another dissident, Shi Tao, who was arrested under conditions very similar to those that led to the arrest of Wang Xiaoning. "This is a real example of why this issue is bigger than any one company and any one industry. All companies must respond in the same way. When a foreign telecommunications company operating in the United States receives an order from U.S. law enforcement, it must comply. Failure to comply in China could have subjected Yahoo! China and its employees to criminal charges, including imprisonment. Ultimately, U.S. companies in China face a choice: comply with Chinese law, or leave."

Yahoo! Is Not Alone

For the most part, U.S. Internet companies doing business in China have agreed to play ball with Beijing. Among the most notable has been Google, the iconic search engine and Internet technology company. Despite its corporate motto of "Don't be evil," in January of 2006 the company voluntarily launched a new search engine for China—www.google.cn—that was compliant with Chinese demands for censorship. "To obey

China's censorship laws, Google's representatives explained, the company had agreed to purge its search results of any Web sites disapproved of by the Chinese government, including Web sites promoting Falun Gong, a government-banned spiritual movement; sites promoting free speech in China; or any mention of the 1989 Tiananmen Square massacre," the *New York Times* reported in April 2006. "If you search for 'Tibet' or 'Falun Gong' most anywhere in the world on google .com, you'll find thousands of blog entries, news items and chat rooms on Chinese repression. Do the same search inside China on google.cn, and most, if not all, of these links will be gone. Google will have erased them completely."

Google continues to defend its participation in censorship efforts. According to a May 2[, 2007] report in *Network World*, "Google's board of directors has recommended shareholders next week vote down a proposal that would require the company to legally resist government censorship efforts and to notify users when the company is required by governments to censor search results." And Google is not alone. Other companies that have agreed not to breach Beijing's "Great Firewall of China" include Skype (partnered with an Internet firm controlled by billionaire Li Ka-shing, who is linked to the People's Republic of China), Microsoft (which shut down a blog at Beijing's request), and others. According to *Business Week*, "scores of other outfits, both domestic and foreign, have made concessions to China's censors."

How does Beijing pull this off? The answer is fear. "The penalty for noncompliance with censorship regulations can be serious," the *New York Times* noted in 2006. "An American public-relations consultant who recently worked for a major domestic Chinese portal recalled an afternoon when Chinese police officers burst into the company's offices, dragged the CEO into a conference room and berated him for failing to block illicit content. 'He was pale with fear afterward,' she said. 'You have to understand, these people are terrified, just terrified. They're seriously worried about slipping up and going to jail. They think about it every day they go into the office."'

If [American] companies are willing to sell out to an authoritarian regime overseas, is it reasonable to assume that they will exhibit any great fidelity to constitutional principles at home?

For harried Americans, beset with innumerable demands on their time and with plenty to worry about in domestic policies and politics, Internet-enabled oppression in China may seem far away and almost academic. Sure, the imprisonment of Wang Xiaoning is tragic and unjust. But that kind of behavior can be expected of a communist country, right?

Still, the participation of American firms in enabling oppression in China is immensely troubling. If these companies are willing to sell out to an authoritarian regime overseas, is it reasonable to assume that they will exhibit any great fidelity to constitutional principles at home?

In fact, U.S. companies have already been helping U.S. federal agencies conduct domestic surveillance. There is, for instance, a class-action lawsuit pending against telecommunications giant AT&T accusing the company of helping the National Security Agency illegally wiretap Americans' communications. Moreover, major Internet firms including Microsoft, AOL, Yahoo!, and Google were subpoenaed by the Justice Department in an attempt to get the companies to turn over details of user search-engine queries. All but Google complied in one fashion or another, though it is unclear how much user data was eventually turned over to the Justice Department. To Google's credit this time, the company fought the subpoena and won in an important privacy victory for users of the world's most popular search engine.

Taken as a whole, however, the picture of corporate behavior, whether in China or at home, is not encouraging. Clearly, corporate elitists have been willing to sell out both at home and abroad if it helps improve the bottom line—and the losers are ordinary citizens who live where freedom and liberty are increasingly rare commodities.

12

Chinese Violation of Intellectual Property Rights Costs U.S. Firms Money

Wayne M. Morrison

Wayne M. Morrison specializes in international trade and finance for the Congressional Research Service, a division of the Library of Congress that provides the U.S. House and Senate with nonpartisan public-policy analysis.

A major issue that has affected trade between the U.S. and China is the violation of intellectual property rights by Chinese manufacturers. Counterfeit products make up as much as one-fifth of the goods made in China, and their sales cost U.S. firms more than $3 billion each year. The Chinese government has not always been willing to enforce laws against pirated materials, though it has been taking important steps such as seizing illegal products and expanding the scope of legitimate licensing. However, more work still needs to be done.

U.S.-China trade rose rapidly after the two nations established diplomatic relations (January 1979), signed a bilateral trade agreement (July 1979), and provided mutual most-favored-nation treatment beginning in 1980. Total trade (exports plus imports) between the two nations rose from about $5 billion in 1980 to $231 billion in 2004; China is now the third-largest U.S. trading partner. Over the past few years,

Wayne M. Morrison, "China-U.S. Trade Issues," *CRS Issue Brief for Congress*, July 1, 2005, pp. 1, 11–13. The Library of Congress.
U.S. trade with China has grown at a faster pace than that of any other major U.S. trading partner. . . .

The United States has pressed China to improve its IPR [intellectual property rights] protection regime since the late 1980s. In 1991, the United States (under a Section 301 case) threatened to impose $1.5 billion in trade sanctions against China if it failed to strengthen its IPR laws. Although China later implemented a number of new IPR laws, it often failed to enforce them, which led the United States to once again threaten China with trade sanctions. The two sides reached a trade agreement in 1995, which pledged China to take immediate steps to stem IPR piracy by cracking down on large-scale producers and distributors of pirated materials and prohibiting the export of pirated products, establishing mechanisms to ensure long-term enforcement of IPR laws and providing greater market access to U.S. IPR-related products.

China Is Not Enforcing Intellectual Property Laws

Under the terms of China's WTO [World Trade Organization] accession, China agreed to immediately bring its IPR laws in compliance with the WTO agreement on Trade Related Aspects of Intellectual Property Rights (TRIPS). The USTR [United States Trade Representative] has stated on a number of occasions that China has made great strides in improving its IPR protection regime, noting that it has passed several new IPR-related laws, closed or fined several assembly operations for illegal production lines, seized millions of illegal audio-visual products, curtailed exports of pirated products, expanded training of judges and law enforcement officials on IPR protection, and expanded legitimate licensing of film and music production in China. However, the USTR has indicated that much work needs to be done to improve China's IPR protection regime. U.S. business groups continue to complain about significant IPR problems in China, especially of illegal reproduction of software, retail piracy, and trademark counterfeiting. It is estimated that counterfeits constitute between

15% and 20% of all products made in China and totals and accounts for about 8% of China's GDP [gross domestic product]. Chinese enforcement agencies and judicial system often lack the resources (or the will) needed to vigorously enforce IPR laws; convicted IPR offenders generally face minor penalties. In addition, while market access for IPR-related products has improved, high tariffs, quotas, and other barriers continue to hamper U.S. exports; such trade barriers are believed to be partly responsible for illegal IPR-related smuggling and counterfeiting in China. Industry analysts estimate that IPR piracy in China cost U.S. copyright firms $2.5 billion to $3.5 billion in lost sales in 2004. The piracy rate for IPR-related products in China (such as motion pictures, software, and sound recordings) is estimated at 90% or higher. In addition, China accounts for a significant share of imported counterfeit products seized by U.S. Customs and Border Protection ($62.5 million, or 66% of total goods seized, in FY2003).

IPR protection has become [one] of the most important bilateral trade issues between the United States and China in recent years:

- In April 2004, the Chinese government pledged to "significantly reduce" IPR infringement levels by increasing efforts to halt production, imports, and sales of counterfeit goods and lowering the threshold for criminal prosecution of IPR violations.

- On November 19, 2004, eight members of the House Ways and Means Committee sent a letter to the Chinese Ambassador to the United States (Yang Jiechi) expressing concern that proposed Chinese regulations on government procurement of software would virtually lock out U.S. software companies due to requirements for local content and technology transfer.

- On December 16, 2004, General Motors Daewoo Auto & Technology Company (a division of General Motors) filed a case in China against Chery Automobile Co. Ltd. (a Chinese firm) for allegedly violating its intellectual property rights by copying one of its car models (the Chevrolet Spark) to produce the Chery QQ. The case has generated further interest in the United States because Chery is planning to export its vehicles to the United States beginning in 2007.

- On February 9, 2005, the International Intellectual Property Alliance and the U.S. Chamber of Commerce urged the USTR to initiate WTO consultations with China for its poor record on IPR enforcement, which could lead the United States to pursue a dispute resolution case against China in the WTO.

On April 29, 2005, the USTR announced that it had placed China on the Special 301 Priority Watch List, due to "serious concerns" over China's compliance with its WTO IPR obligations and China's failure to fully implement its pledges on IPR made in April 2004 to make a significant reduction in IPR piracy. The USTR urged China to launch more criminal piracy cases and to improve market access for IPR-related products and warned that it was considering taking a case to the WTO if IPR enforcement does not show significant improvement soon. U.S. officials have asked China to provide detailed statistics on IPR enforcement effort to determine if China's recent enforcement effort is making a difference in bringing down piracy levels. IPR will likely be a major issue when the United States and China meet under the auspices of the U.S.-China Joint Committee on Commerce and Trade (JCCT) on July 11, 2005. [China pledged to improve its enforcement of antipiracy laws.]

13

China's Economic Growth Is Bad for the Environment

Joseph Kahn and Jim Yardley

Joseph Kahn is a journalist for the International Herald Tribune *and the Beijing bureau chief for the* New York Times. *Jim Yardley is a Pulitzer Prize-winning journalist.*

The emergence of China as a major industrial power has had devastating effects on its environment. Water and air pollution affects much of the nation, especially in the cities, and causes hundreds of thousands of deaths annually. This pollution has caused international problems as well. The Chinese government needs to make fundamental changes to improve the nation's environment, but it is unwilling to do so at the expense of its economy.

No country in history has emerged as a major industrial power without creating a legacy of environmental damage that can take decades and big dollops of public wealth to undo.

But just as the speed and scale of the rise of China as an economic power have no clear parallel in history, so its pollution problem has shattered all precedents. Environmental degradation in China is so severe, with such stark domestic and international repercussions, that pollution poses not only a major long-term burden on the Chinese public but also an acute political challenge to the ruling Communist Party. And it is not clear that China can rein in its own economic juggernaut.

Joseph Kahn and Jim Yardley, "The Dark Side of China's Boom," *International Herald Tribune*, August 27, 2007, p. 1. Copyright © 1997 by The New York Times Company. Reprinted with permission.

Public health is reeling. Pollution has made cancer the leading cause of death in China, the Chinese Ministry of Health says. Ambient air pollution alone is blamed for hundreds of thousands of deaths each year. Nearly 500 million people lack access to safe drinking water.

An Environmental Catastrophe

Chinese cities often seem wrapped in a toxic gray shroud. Only 1 percent of the 560 million Chinese city dwellers breathe air considered safe by the European Union. Beijing is frantically searching for a magic formula, a meteorological deus ex machina, to clear its skies for the 2008 Olympics.

Environmental woes that might be considered catastrophic in some countries can seem commonplace in China: industrial cities where people rarely see the sun; children killed or sickened by lead poisoning or other types of local pollution; a coastline so swamped by algal red tides that large sections of the ocean no longer sustain marine life.

China is choking on its own success. The economy is on a historic run, posting a succession of double-digit growth rates. But the growth derives, now more than at any time in the recent past, from a staggering expansion of heavy industry and urbanization that requires colossal inputs of energy, almost all from coal, the most readily available, and dirtiest, source.

"It is a very awkward situation for the country because our greatest achievement is also our biggest burden," said Wang Jinnan, one of the leading environmental researchers in China. "There is pressure for change, but many people refuse to accept that we need a new approach so soon."

The problem of China has become the world's problem. Sulfur dioxide and nitrogen oxides spewed by Chinese coal-fired power plants fall as acid rain on Seoul and Tokyo. Much of the particulate pollution over Los Angeles originates in China, according to the *Journal of Geophysical Research*.

More pressing still, China has entered the most robust stage of its industrial revolution, even as much of the outside world has become preoccupied with global warming.

Experts once thought China might overtake the United States as the world's leading producer of greenhouse gases by 2010, possibly later. Now, the International Energy Agency has said China could become the emissions leader by the end of [2007] and the Netherlands Environment Assessment Agency said China had already passed the milestone.

For the Communist Party, the political calculus is daunting.

China's Responses to Pollution

Reining in economic growth to alleviate pollution may seem logical, but the Chinese authoritarian system is addicted to fast growth. Delivering prosperity placates the public, provides spoils for well-connected officials and forestalls demands for political change.

A major slowdown could incite social unrest, alienate business interests and threaten the party's rule.

But pollution poses its own threat. Officials blame fetid air and water for thousands of episodes of social unrest. Health care costs have climbed sharply. Severe water shortages could turn more farmland into desert. And the unconstrained expansion of energy-intensive industries creates greater dependence on imported oil and dirty coal, meaning that environmental problems get harder and more expensive to address the longer they are unresolved.

Chinese leaders recognize that the country must change course. They are vowing to overhaul the growth-first philosophy of the Deng Xiaoping era and embrace a new model that allows for steady growth while protecting the environment. In the equivalent of a State of the Union address this year, Prime

Minister Wen Jiabao made 48 references to "environment," "pollution" or "environmental protection."

The government has numerical targets for reducing emissions and conserving energy. Export subsidies for polluting industries have been phased out. Different campaigns have been started to close illegal coal mines and shutter some heavily polluting factories. Major initiatives are under way to develop clean energy sources like solar and wind power. And environmental regulation in Beijing, Shanghai and other leading cities has been tightened before the 2008 Olympics.

Yet most of the government's targets for energy efficiency, as well as improving air and water quality, have gone unmet. And there are ample signs that the leadership is either unwilling or unable to make fundamental changes.

Land, water, electricity, oil and bank loans remain relatively inexpensive, even for heavy polluters. Beijing has declined to use the kind of tax policies and market-oriented incentives for conservation that have worked well in Japan and many European countries.

Chinese manufacturers who dump waste into rivers or pump smoke into the sky make the cheap products that fill stores in the United States.

Provincial officials, who enjoy substantial autonomy, often ignore environmental edicts, helping to reopen mines or factories closed by the national authorities. Overall, enforcement is often tinged with corruption. In February [2007], the Chinese media reported that officials in Yunnan Province in southern China beautified Laoshou Mountain, which had been used as a quarry, by spraying green paint over hectares of rock.

President Hu Jintao's most ambitious attempt to change the culture of fast-growth collapsed this year. The project, known as "Green GDP," was an effort to create an environmental yardstick for evaluating the performance of every official in China. It recalculated gross domestic product, or GDP, to reflect the cost of pollution.

But the early results were so sobering—in some provinces the pollution-adjusted economic growth rates were reduced almost to zero—that the project was banished to China's ivory tower this spring and stripped of official influence.

Pollution and Prosperity

Chinese leaders argue that the outside world is a partner in degrading the environment of China. Chinese manufacturers who dump waste into rivers or pump smoke into the sky make the cheap products that fill stores in the United States and Europe. Often, these manufacturers subcontract for foreign companies—or are owned by them.

Foreign investment continues to rise as multinational corporations build more factories in China. Beijing also insists that it will accept no mandatory limits on its carbon dioxide emissions, which would almost certainly reduce its industrial growth. It argues that rich countries caused global warming and should find a way to solve it without impinging on the economic development of China.

Indeed, Britain, the United States and Japan polluted their way to prosperity and worried about environmental damage only after their economies matured and their urban middle classes demanded blue skies and safe drinking water.

But China is more like a teenage smoker with emphysema. The costs of pollution have mounted well before it is ready to curtail economic development. But the price of business as usual—including the predicted effects of global warming on China itself—strikes many of its own experts and some senior officials as intolerably high.

"Typically, industrial countries deal with green problems when they are rich," said Ren Yong, a climate expert at the

Center for Environment and Economy in Beijing. "We have to deal with them while we are still poor. There is no model for us to follow."

In the face of past challenges, the Communist Party has usually responded with sweeping edicts from Beijing. Some environmentalists say they hope the top leadership has now made pollution control such a high priority that lower-level officials will have no choice but to go along, just as Deng once forced the sluggish Chinese bureaucracy to fixate on economic growth.

But the environment may end up posing a different political challenge. A command-and-control political culture accustomed to issuing thundering directives is under pressure, even from people in the ruling party, to submit to oversight from the public, for which pollution has become a daily—and increasingly deadly—reality.

The Degradation of Air, Land, and Water

During the three decades since Deng set China on a course toward market-style growth, rapid industrialization and urbanization have lifted hundreds of millions of Chinese out of poverty and made the country the world's largest producer of consumer goods. But there is little question that growth came at the expense of the air, land and water, much of it already degraded by decades of Stalinist economic planning that emphasized the development of heavy industries in urban areas.

For air quality, a major culprit is coal, on which China relies for about two-thirds of its surging energy needs. It has abundant supplies of coal and already burns more of it than the United States, Europe and Japan combined. But even many of its newest coal-fired power plants and industrial furnaces operate inefficiently and use pollution controls considered inadequate in the West.

Expanding car ownership, heavy traffic and low-grade gasoline have made automobiles the leading source of air pollution in major Chinese cities.

One major pollutant contributing to the polluted air is particulate matter, which includes concentrations of fine dust, soot and aerosol particles less than 10 microns in diameter, known as PM 10.

The level of such particulates is measured in micrograms per cubic meter of air. The European Union stipulates that any reading above 40 micrograms is unsafe. The United States allows 50. In 2006, the average PM 10 level in Beijing was 141, according to the Chinese National Bureau of Statistics. Only Cairo, among world capitals, had worse air quality as measured by particulates, according to the World Bank.

Emissions of sulfur dioxide from coal and fuel oil, which can cause respiratory and cardiovascular diseases as well as acid rain, are increasing even faster than Chinese economic growth. In 2005, China became the leading source of sulfur dioxide pollution globally, the State Environmental Protection Administration reported [in 2006].

Other major air pollutants, including ozone, an important component of smog, and smaller particulate matter, called PM 2.5, emitted when gasoline is burned, are not widely monitored in China. Medical experts in China and in the West have argued that PM 2.5 causes more chronic diseases of the lung and heart than the more widely watched PM 10.

A Lack of Water Conservation

Perhaps an even more acute challenge is water. China has only one-fifth as much water per capita as the United States. But while southern China is relatively wet, the north, home to about half of the Chinese population, is an immense, parched region that now threatens to become the world's biggest desert.

Farmers in the north once used shovels to dig their wells. Now, many aquifers have been so depleted that some wells in

Beijing and Hebei Province must extend more than 800 meters, or half a mile, before they reach fresh water.

Industry and agriculture use nearly all of the flow of the Yellow River before it reaches the Bohai Sea.

In response, Chinese leaders have undertaken one of the most ambitious engineering projects in world history, a $60 billion network of canals, rivers and lakes to transport water from the flood-prone Yangtze River to the silt-choked Yellow River. But that effort, if successful, will still leave the north chronically thirsty.

This scarcity has not yet created a culture of conservation. Water remains inexpensive by global standards, and Chinese industry uses 4 to 10 times more water per unit of production than the average in industrialized nations, according to the World Bank.

China has come to rely mainly on energy-intensive heavy industry and urbanization to fuel economic growth.

In many parts of China, factories and farms dump waste into surface water with few legal repercussions. Chinese environmental monitors say that one-third of all river water, and vast sections of the great lakes of China, the Tai, Chao and Dianchi, have water rated Grade V, the most degraded level, rendering it unfit for industrial or agricultural use. . . .

A Worsening Picture

As gloomy as the Chinese pollution picture looks, it is set to get significantly worse, because China has come to rely mainly on energy-intensive heavy industry and urbanization to fuel economic growth.

In 2000, a team of economists and energy specialists at the Development Research Center, part of the Chinese State Council, set out to gauge how much energy China would need over the ensuing 20 years to achieve the leadership's goal of quadrupling the size of the economy.

They based their projections on the first 20 years of Chinese economic reform, from 1980 to 2000. In that period, China relied mainly on light industry and small-scale private enterprise to spur growth. It made big improvements in energy efficiency even as the economy expanded rapidly. Gross domestic product quadrupled, while energy use only doubled.

The team projected that such efficiency gains would probably continue. But the experts also offered what they called a worst-case situation in which the most energy-hungry parts of the economy grew faster and efficiency gains fell short.

That worst-case situation now looks wildly optimistic. [In 2006,] China burned the energy equivalent of 2.7 billion tons of coal, three-quarters of what the experts had said would be the maximum required in 2020. To put it another way, China seems likely to need as much energy in 2010 as it thought it would need in 2020 under the most pessimistic assumptions.

"No one really knew what was driving the economy, which is why the predictions were so wrong," said Yang Fuqiang, a former Chinese energy planner who is now the chief China representative of the Energy Foundation, an American group that supports energy-related research. "What I fear is that the trend is now basically irreversible."

The ravenous appetite for fossil fuels traces partly to an economic stimulus program in 1997. The leadership, worried that the Chinese economy would fall into a steep recession as its East Asian neighbors had, provided generous state financing and tax incentives to support industrialization on a grand scale.

It worked well, possibly too well. In 1996, China and the United States each accounted for 13 percent of global steel production. By 2005, the United States share had dropped to 8 percent, while China's share had risen to 35 percent, according to a study by Daniel Rosen and Trevor Houser of China Strategic Advisory, a group that analyzes the Chinese economy.

Similarly, China now makes half of the world's cement and flat glass, and about a third of its aluminum. In 2006, China overtook Japan as the second-largest market for cars and trucks after the United States.

Inefficient Energy Use

Its energy needs are compounded because even some of its newest heavy industry plants do not operate as efficiently—or control pollution as effectively—as factories in other parts of the world, according to a recent World Bank report.

The Chinese aluminum industry alone consumes as much energy as the country's commercial sector.

Chinese steel makers, on average, use one-fifth more energy per ton than the international average. Cement manufacturers need 45 percent more power, and ethylene producers need 70 percent more than producers elsewhere, the World Bank said.

The Chinese aluminum industry alone consumes as much energy as the country's commercial sector—all the hotels, restaurants, banks and shopping malls combined, Rosen and Houser reported.

Moreover, the boom is not limited to heavy industry. Each year for the past few years, China has built about 700 million square meters, or 7.5 billion square feet, of commercial and residential space, more than the combined floor space of all the shopping malls and strip malls in the United States, according to data collected by the U.S. Energy Information Administration.

Chinese buildings rarely have thermal insulation. They require, on average, twice as much energy to heat and cool as those in similar climates in the United States and Europe, according to the World Bank.

The vast majority of new buildings—95 percent, the bank says—do not meet Chinese codes for energy efficiency.

All these new buildings require China to build power plants, which it has been doing prodigiously. In 2005 alone, China added 66 gigawatts of electrical generating capacity to its power grid, about as much power as Britain generates in a year. [In 2006,] it added an additional 102 gigawatts, about as much as France.

This increase has come almost entirely from small and medium-size coal-fired power plants that were built quickly and inexpensively.

Only a few of them use modern, combined-cycle turbines, which increase efficiency, said Noureddine Berrah, an energy expert at the World Bank. He said Beijing had so far declined to use the most advanced type of combined-cycle turbines despite having completed a successful pilot project nearly a decade ago.

While over the long term, combined-cycle plants save money and reduce pollution, Berrah said, they cost more and take longer to build. For that reason, he said, national and provincial government officials prefer older technology.

"China is making decisions today that will affect its energy use for the next 30 or 40 years," he said. "Unfortunately, in some parts of the government the thinking is much more shortsighted."

14

Education Must Improve for the U.S. to Compete Economically with China

William T. Archey

Archey is the president and chief executive officer of the American Electronics Association.

China is catching up to the United States in terms of technology. For example, China graduates four times as many engineers as the United States and is America's biggest trading partner for technology products. America risks falling behind China and other nations, particularly Asian nations, if it does not increase funding for research and development and improve the skills of its workforce by teaching vital math and science skills in the K–12 school system.

M r. Chairman and distinguished Members of the Commission, thank you for having me here today to talk with you about the topic of U.S. competitiveness. This is a very timely discussion as I just returned from a weeklong trip in China. This was my 22nd trip to China. My first trip was in 1981 to Beijing. I refer to that period as the "BT" period. Before Traffic. At that time, a trip across town took 10–15 minutes. Today, it takes an hour or more. The traffic today is emblematic of what is happening in China, and especially Beijing.

In February [2005], AeA [American Electronics Association] released a report whose title says it all: "Losing the Com-

William T. Archey, "China's High Technology Development," Hearing Before the U.S.-China Economic and Security Review Commission One Hundred Ninth Congress, First

Session, April 21–22, 2005, pp. 156–158. www.uscc.gov.
petitive Advantage? The Challenge for Science and Technology in the United States." I am submitting a copy of this report to the Commission for the record.

The thrust of our report is that the United States is slipping. Yes, we are still the leader in nearly every way that one can measure, but that lead is eroding as other countries are catching up.

The United States Is Facing Economic Competition

Let me be clear, it isn't that the United States is in decline. It's that others are advancing quickly from behind, putting all their economic resources into moving their countries forward. The problem is that even if the United States were doing everything right, the world still poses an unprecedented competitive challenge. Unfortunately, we aren't doing everything right, and this compounds the challenges that we face.

China now graduates four times the number of engineers as the United States.

Our report on competitiveness identified five themes, which the United States needs to address to prevent an impending slide in U.S. global competitiveness.

First, the economic reforms around the world are rapidly transforming economies, making them dramatically more competitive.

The United States has long urged the world to adopt free market principles. Well, the world listened. Major economic reforms have taken place in Russia, Eastern Europe, China, and India, to name a few. Indeed, if you look back just 20 years to 1985, over 60 percent of the world lived under command-and-control economic systems.

While many Americans are just now beginning to recognize how competitive the world has become, this change didn't happen overnight. Just as the U.S. didn't achieve its current leadership overnight. It takes years of investment in your innovation infrastructure. You need to invest in research and development, particularly basic research. You need to invest in your people, especially in science and technology education. You need to adopt a system that encourages investment, welcomes change, and promotes risk-taking and rewards it.

Which brings us to our *second* theme, that other countries are adopting and utilizing technology to enhance their economic growth and competitiveness. And as a recent [as of 2005] CIA [Central Intelligence Agency] report states, "the greatest benefits of globalization [will] accrue to countries and groups that can access and adopt new technologies."

Technology Creates Jobs

Already many countries are using technology to leapfrog from behind. Technology allows countries to bypass traditional development paths and use the latest technology to bring themselves forward. The implications are far reaching for U.S. competitiveness; the stagnant economy of yesterday could be the competitive rival of tomorrow. There is no better example of leapfrogging than the development of China's wireless telecommunications infrastructure.

Other countries realize that the U.S. experience of the 1980s and 1990s is the model to be followed. Namely that the growth of the high-tech sector leads to wealth and job creation. But for that to happen, there is a need to build a high-tech infrastructure.

In 2004, . . . China was the largest U.S. trading partner for technology products.

To this end, many countries are making great strides. China now graduates four times the number of engineers as the United States. Japan graduates twice as many, and South Korea with one-sixth the population, graduates the same number of engineers as we do.

The changes in China have led to massive injections of investment into the Chinese economy, and where investment goes, trade follows. In 2002, China surpassed the United States as the prime destination for foreign direct investment in the world. In 2004, China surpassed the United States as Japan's largest trading partner. In the same year, China was the largest U.S. trading partner for technology products, surpassing the combined 25 countries of the European Union.

China is not alone. Many countries are increasingly climbing the technology ladder. As with China, they are no longer satisfied simply to manufacture technology products. They are also striving to become creators and designers of the next generation of breakthrough technology products and services.

America Must Improve Its Education System

This is my *third* point. If U.S. workers are to compete in a world economy that is increasingly knowledge based and driven by technology, the American education system must improve.

A highly skilled workforce is the lifeblood of any successful company, industry, or national economy. Regrettably, the American K–12 system is failing to provide the math and science skills necessary for kids to compete in the 21st century workforce. Which in turn means that the U.S. higher education system cannot produce enough scientists and engineers to support the growth of the U.S. high-tech industry that is so crucial to our economic prosperity.

We should be appalled and embarrassed that our 12th-graders score at the bottom on international math and science tests. Far too often, our students shy away from engineering and tech programs because these are seen as careers for geeks and nerds. Interestingly in China, 39 percent of its college students are majoring in engineering while only five percent do so in the United States.

This leads me to my *fourth* point. If we cannot produce enough domestic scientists and engineers, keeping out high-skilled foreign talent is not the answer.

For decades, if not centuries, America has been the beneficiary of an influx of many of the most talented minds on this planet. Foreign-born individuals represent one of every five scientists and engineers in the United States. That is over 1 million workers. These workers are job creators. They contribute a tremendous amount of knowledge, talent, and innovation to the U.S. economy. People might be surprised to learn that almost half of the Nobel Prizes awarded to researchers in the United States between 1901 and 1991 were won by foreign-born individuals or their children.

Unfortunately, immigration policy post 9/11 has deterred foreign nationals from coming to the United States to study or work at the very time that this talent has tremendous opportunities elsewhere. We literally cannot afford to lose their intellectual abilities. Indeed, last year we saw a 35 percent decline in Chinese applications to U.S. graduate schools of engineering.

Finally, the U.S. federal funding that spawned so many technology breakthroughs in the 20th century is faltering. Few people realize that federal funding helped create the Internet, MRI scanners, the mouse, and GPS system—to name a very select few.

So what has been happening to R&D funding? Well, federally funded research has declined as a portion of the economy, and the priorities have shifted away from technology. In 1981, half of all federal R&D went to technology; by 2003 this dropped to one-third.

In November 2004, the U.S. Congress even cut the budget of the National Science Foundation by $105 million, the first cut in 16 years.

Government investment plays an indispensable role in building the foundation of a knowledge-based economy by investing in ventures, concepts, and ideas often years before a commercially viable product or service is available. When government provides the foundation, U.S. businesses convert these innovations into new products, services, and sometimes, new industries. Why would we want to break this cycle?

A Precarious Lead

Mr. Chairman, the United States is not preordained to lead the world in economic or technological advancement. We achieved this lead by the sweat of our brow and 60 years of investments in our infrastructure. We understood that innovation—taken in its broadest sense as the open acceptance of change and new ideas—is what fuels our economy.

Yes, we are still in the lead, but I hope that everyone understands that it is a precarious one. While we are taking this lead for granted, others are rapidly moving up from behind.

The world is a changed environment. It is intensely more competitive, and we are going to have to work harder to stay out front. Unless this realization hits home, our lead will continue to narrow, and at some point, we will be staring at someone else's back.

Mr. Chairman and Members of the Commission, thank you for having me here today.

Organizations to Contact

The editors have compiled the following list of organizations concerned with the issues debated in this book. The descriptions are derived from materials provided by the organizations. All have publications or information available for interested readers. The list was compiled on the date of publication of the present volume; the information provided here may change. Be aware that many organizations take several weeks or longer to respond to inquiries, so allow as much time as possible.

American Chamber of Commerce in the People's Republic of China
China Resources Building, Suite 1903
No. 8 Jianguomenbei Avenue, Beijing 100005
  China
(8610) 8519-1920 • fax: (8610) 8519-1910
e-mail: amcham@amcham-china.org.cn
Web site: www.amcham-china.org.cn

The chamber is a nonprofit organization that represents American individuals and companies that do business with China. It uses advocacy and education to help American companies succeed in China. The chamber operates a number of committees, including ones on corporate social responsibility and U.S. government relations. Articles from its monthly magazine *China Brief* are available on its Web site.

Amnesty International
5 Penn Plaza, Sixteenth Floor, New York, NY 10001
(212) 807-8400 • fax: (212) 463-9193
e-mail: admin-us@aiusa.org
Web site: www.amnesty.org

Amnesty International is an international organization that promotes human rights. In 1999 it launched the "China: Ten Years After Tiananmen" campaign to raise awareness of the imprisonment of political dissidents in China. Details of the campaign are available on the group's Web site. Amnesty International also publishes an annual report detailing human rights violations around the globe. Reports on China available on the Web site include "China's Growing Underclass" and "Undermining Freedom of Expression in China: The Role of Yahoo!"

Brookings Institution

1775 Massachusetts Avenue, NW
Washington, DC 20036-2188
(202) 797-6000
Web site: www.brookings.edu

The institution is a private, nonprofit organization devoted to research, education, and publication in economics, business, government, foreign policy, and the social sciences. Its principal purpose is to contribute informed perspectives on the current and emerging public-policy issues facing the American people. Its publications include journals and books. Research and commentary on China, such as "Debunking the China Syndrome," is available on the Web site.

Cato Institute

1000 Massachusetts Avenue, NW
Washington, DC 20001-5403
(202) 842-0200 • fax: (202) 842-3490
Web site: www.cato.org

The Cato Institute is a nonpartisan public-policy research organization that promotes the principles of limited government, individual liberty, and peace. Relations with China are a major research area within the institute's Center for Trade Policy Studies. The institute publishes policy analysis reports and op-eds, including "U.S.-China Relations: The Case for Economic Liberalism" and "Free Markets, Not Protectionism, Key to Chinese Economic Reform."

Freedom House

1301 Connecticut Avenue, NW, Floor 6
Washington, D.C.   20036
(202) 296-5101 • fax: (202) 293-2840
e-mail: info@freedomhouse.org
Web site: www.freedomhouse.org

Freedom House promotes human rights, democracy, free market economics, the rule of law, and independent media around the world. It publishes *Freedom in the World*, an annual comparative assessment of the state of political rights and civil liberties in 191 countries. A report on China is available on the Web site.

Human Rights in China

350 5th Avenue, Suite 3311, New York, NY   10118
(212) 239-4495 • fax: (212) 239-2561
e-mail: hrichina@hrichina.org
Web site: www.hrichina.org

Human Rights in China (HRIC) is an international nongovernmental organization founded by Chinese scientists and scholars. It monitors the implementation of international human rights standards in the People's Republic of China and carries out human rights advocacy and education among Chinese people inside and outside the country. HRIC also addresses issues such as freedom of expression. Its publications include *China Rights Forum* as well as books, videos, and reports on the status of human rights in China.

Human Rights Watch

350 5th Avenue, 34th Floor, New York, NY   10118-3299
(212) 290-4700 • fax: (212) 736-1300
e-mail: hrwnyc@hrw.org
Web site: www.hrw.org

The goal of Human Rights Watch, an international advocacy organization, is to raise awareness about human rights and to investigate and expose human rights violations. It publishes annual reports as well as special reports on China, such as "Race to the Bottom: Corporate Complicity in Chinese Internet Censorship" and "Paying the Price: Worker Unrest in Northeast China."

International Labour Office

4 route des Morillons, Geneva 22   CH-1211
  Switzerland
+41.22.799.6111 • fax: +41.22.798.8685
e-mail: ilo@ilo.org or washington@ilo.org
Web site: www.ilo.org

The International Labour Office (ILO) works to promote basic human rights through improved working and living conditions by enhancing opportunities for those who are excluded from meaningful salaried employment. The ILO pioneered such landmarks of industrial society as the eight-hour work day, maternity protection, and workplace safety regulations. It runs the ILO Publications Bureau, which publishes policy statements and background information on all aspects of employment; among these publications are reports on forced labor and corporate social responsibility.

Laogai Research Foundation

1109 M Street, NW, Washington, DC   20005
(202) 408-8300 • fax: (202) 408-8302
e-mail: laogai@laogai.org
Web site: www.laogai.org

Founded by human rights activist Harry Wu, the foundation is dedicated to collecting information about China's system of forced-labor camps. The Web site features news stories and publications, such as the *Laogai Handbook*.

National Committee on United States-China Relations (NCUSCR)

71 West 23rd Street, Suite 1901, New York, NY   10010-4102
(212) 645-9677 • fax: (212) 645-1695

e-mail: info@ncuscr.org
Web site: www.ncuscr.org

Established in 1966, the NCUSCR is dedicated to creating a productive relationship between the United States and China. The committee works to achieve this goal by increasing the dialogue between Americans and Chinese through techniques such as an exchange student program and trips to China for American politicians. The organization publishes an annual report and a newsletter.

The US-China Business Council
1818 N Street, NW, Suite 200, Washington, DC   20036-2470
(202) 429-0340 • fax: (202) 775-2476
E-mail: info@uschina.org
Web site: www.uschina.org

The US-China Business Council is a nonprofit organization of more than 250 U.S. corporations that do business with China. The council supports efforts that benefit the U.S. economy, such as lifting trade barriers. The council publishes the bi-monthly magazine *China Business Review*, newsletters, and reports on issues such as consumer safety and corporate social responsibility.

U.S.-China Economic and Security Review Commission
444 North Capitol Street, NW, Suite 602
Washington, DC   20001
(202) 624-1407
e-mail: contact@uscc.gov
Web site: www.uscc.gov

The commission consists of twelve people, appointed in equal numbers by the majority and minority leaders of the U.S. Senate, the Speaker of the House of Representatives, and the minority leader of the House. The purpose of the commission is to monitor the national security implications of the economic ties between the United States and China and to make recommendations to Congress. Reports, speeches, and congressional testimony are available on the Web site.

Bibliography

Books

Ilan Alon and John R. McIntyre, eds. *Globalization of Chinese Enterprises.* New York: Palgrave Macmillan, 2008.

Sara Bongiorni *A Year Without "Made in China": One Family's True Life Adventure in the Global Economy.* Hoboken, NJ: Wiley, 2007.

Elizabeth C. Economy *The River Runs Black: The Environmental Challenge to China's Future.* Ithaca, NY: Cornell University Press, 2005.

Ted C. Fishman *China, Inc.: How the Rise of the Next Superpower Challenges America and the World.* New York: Scribner, 2005.

Thomas L. Friedman *The World Is Flat: A Brief History of the Twenty-First Century.* New York: Farrar, Straus and Giroux, 2006.

Ethan Gutmann *Losing the New China: A Story of American Commerce, Desire, and Betrayal.* San Francisco: Encounter Books, 2004.

W. John Hoffman and Michael Enright *China into the Future: Making Sense of the World's Most Dynamic Economy.* Hoboken, NJ: Wiley, 2008.

Will Hutton | *The Writing on the Wall: Why We Must Embrace China as a Partner or Face It as an Enemy.* New York: Free Press, 2006.

James Kynge | *China Shakes the World: A Titan's Rise and Troubled Future—and the Challenge for America.* Boston: Mariner Books, 2007.

Ben Mah | *America and China: Political and Economic Relations in the 21st Century.* Bloomington, IN: iUniverse, 2007.

James Mann | *The China Fantasy: How Our Leaders Explain Away Chinese Repression.* New York: Viking, 2007.

Joseph E. Stiglitz | *Making Globalization Work.* New York: Norton, 2006.

Yongnian Zheng | *Technological Empowerment: The Internet, State, and Society in China.* Stanford, CA: Stanford University Press, 2008.

Periodicals

Brian Bremner | "China's Big, Dirty Secret," *Business Week Online,* February 1, 2005.

Tyler Cowen | "China Is Big Trouble for the U.S. Balance of Trade, Right? Well, Not So Fast," *New York Times,* September 7, 2006.

Daniel W. Drezner | "The Outsourcing Bogeyman," *Foreign Affairs,* May/June 2004.

Economist	"Here Be Dragons: Search Engines," January 28, 2006.
Economist	"Lost in Translation," May 17, 2007.
James Fallows	"China Makes, the World Takes," *Atlantic Monthly*, July/August 2007.
Aaron L. Friedberg	"Are We Ready for China?" *Commentary*, October 2007.
Christina Larson	"The Green Leap Forward," *Washington Monthly*, July/August 2007.
Don Lee	"China Marches into Outsourcing," *Los Angeles Times*, April 8, 2008.
Steve Maich	"China and the Great Silent Recession," *Maclean's*, March 24, 2008.
Rick Newman	"Made in China: Should You Worry?" *U.S. News and World Report*, July 13, 2007.
James Pethokoukis	"China's Global Reach," *U.S. News & World Report*, August 6, 2007.
Bill Powell	"China's At-Risk Factories," *Time*, April 28, 2008.
Kirk Shink	"China's Great Leap Elevates the Risk," *U.S. News & World Report*, January 14, 2008.
Jim Yardley	"Choking on Progress," *New York Times*, January 9, 2006.

Index

U.S. Senate Commerce Subcommittee on Interstate Commerce and Trade, 61
U.S. Senate Democrats, 59
U.S.-South Korea Free Trade Agreement, 15
U.S. Trade Representative (USTR), 21, 86, 88

V

Vallese, Julie, 52, 55
Village elections, 35
Voice of America, 76

W

Wal-Mart, 58, 67
Wang Jinnan, 90
Wang Xiaoning, 77–81
Water
  aquifers, 95
  pollution, 75, 90, 95–96
Weekly Standard (magazine), 73
Wen Jiabao, 91
Wired News (online magazine), 77
Wireless telecommunications, 102
Wolfson, Scott J., 52
Workers' unions, 66–68, 70, 71
Working-class Americans, 36
World Bank, 98, 99
World economic reforms, 101–102
World Organization for Human Rights USA, 78
World trade competition, 105

World Trade Organization
  China's membership in, 24, 26–27, 31
  currency manipulation control and, 14, 21
  Intellectual property laws and, 20, 86, 88
  laws of, on China, 26–27
  tariffs position, 13
Wu, Harry, 61, 109
Wyden, Ron, 27–28
Wyman, Taylor, 23

Y

Yahoo!, 24, 33, 76, 78, 79–81, 83
Yang Fuqiang, 97
Yang Jiechi, 87
Yangtze River, 96
Yardley, Jim, 89
Yellow River, 96
Ying Ma, 73
Yo-yo water balls, 56–57
Yong, Ren, 93
Yu Ling, 77, 78, 79
Yunnan Province, 92

Z

Zhang, Jacqueline, 7
Zhejiang Province, 63
Zheng Xiaovu, 9, 10, 18
Zimbabwe, 33